Easy-to-Use • Easy-to-Carry
The Essential Playing Companion

Jake Jackson

FLAME TREE
PUBLISHING

Publisher and Creative Director: Nick Wells
Text, Design & Notation: Jake Jackson

Special thanks to Laura Bulbeck and Chris Herbert

14 16 18 17 15
1 3 5 7 9 10 8 6 4 2

This edition first published 2014 by
FLAME TREE PUBLISHING
Crabtree Hall, Crabtree Lane
Fulham, London SW6 6TY
United Kingdom
www.flametreepublishing.com

Music website: www.flametreemusic.com

ISBN 978-1-78361-316-8

A CIP record for this book is available from the British Library upon request.

Acknowledgements
All images and notation courtesy of
Jake Jackson/Flame Tree Publishing Ltd.

Jake Jackson is a musician and writer of practical music books. His publications include *Advanced Guitar Chords*; *Beginners Guide to Reading Music*; *Chords for Kids*; *Classic Riffs*; *Guitar Chords*; *How to Play Electric Guitar*; *Piano and Keyboard Chords*; *Scales and Modes* and *The Songwriter's Rhyming Dictionary*.

Printed in China

Contents

About this Book

Learning to play the ukulele can be fun and rewarding. Playing on your own, with friends, listening and playing along to songs, the ukulele is a great instrument to pick up and play.

The quickest way to start is to learn some chords. Chords are the building blocks of all musical compositions so we've tried to make the following pages as straightforward as possible, so you can start to play straightaway.

The book is organised by key and offers you plenty of information to help you build your understanding. Each chord is clearly laid out, giving you the musical spelling, and the notes on each string of the instrument.

When you've learned the basics, you can start to practise chord shapes, and moving from one chord to the next.

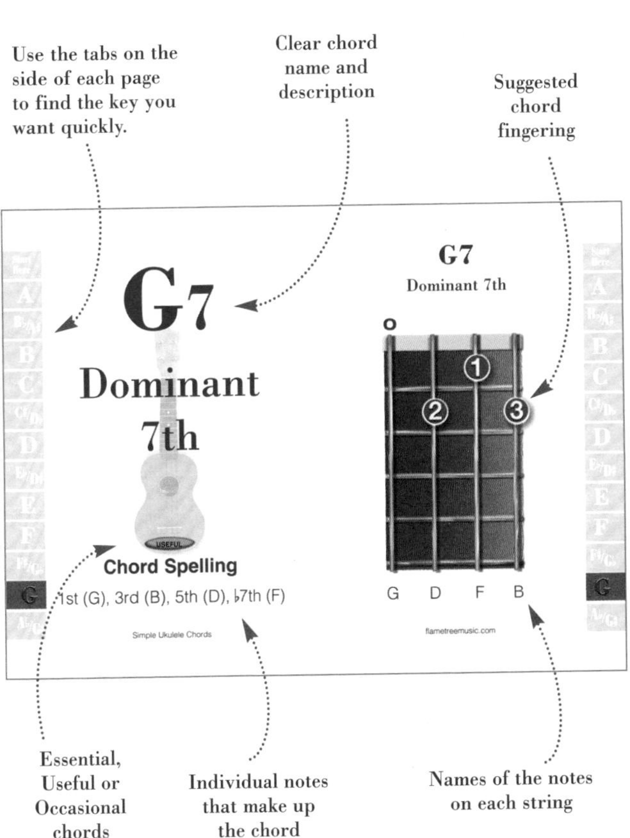

Start Here
A
B♭/A♯
B
C
C♯/D♭
D
E♭/D♯
E
F
F♯/G♭
G
A♭/G♯

How to Use the Chord Diagrams

The chord diagrams (or chord boxes, or fretboxes) in this book will help you to learn the shapes of hundreds of chords, and will be a useful reference guide. This is not comprehensive, but more than enough to play every popular song, in most musical styles, from pop to rock, folk, blues and country!

Triads are basic three-note chords. There are four basic triads: a **major** triad is the **first**, **third** and **fifth** notes of the diatonic **major scale** (C, E and G in the key of C); a **minor** triad is the **first**, **third** and **fifth** notes of the natural minor scale; an **augmented triad** is a major triad with a **sharpened fifth note**; and a **diminished triad** is a minor triad with a **flattened fifth note**. All of these basic chords can be extended; a **major seventh chord**, for example, is a **major triad** with a **seventh note added**.

Keys and Structure

The chords are divided by key, from A to G#, with the chord name shown on the left page and at the top of the right hand page.

The left-hand page also shows the **chord spelling**, giving you the musical structure of each chord. A chord is made up of at least three of the 8 positions:

1st 2nd 3rd 4th 5th 6th 7th 8th

Most chords are based on these 8 positions. Simple chords are called triads, ie three notes, usually with the first note indicating the chord:

1st	2nd	**3rd**	4th	**5th**	6th	7th	8th
C		**E**		**G**			

This is the **C major chord**, using the **1st**, **3rd** and **5th** notes of the major scale.

On the ukulele, because of the particular way its strings work, these notes can be played in a number of positions.

We've suggested a common way of representing the chord, but it is worth understanding how the notes work on a fretboard. You can play the same notes in several places, and play the note either an octave above or below. This becomes especially useful when playing with others so that you create a wider, more interesting sound.

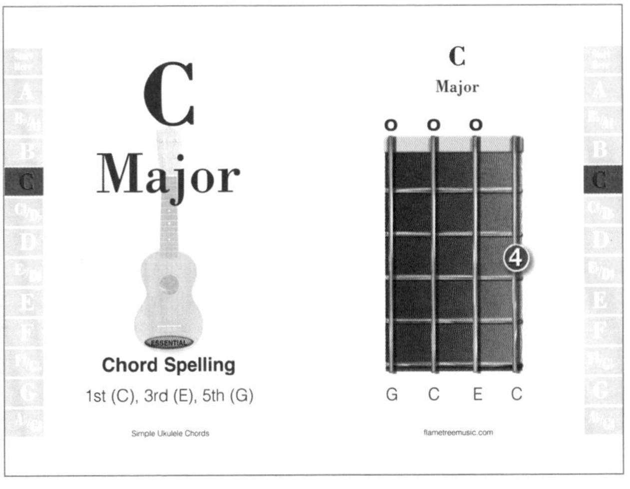

Some chords use a flattened 3rd, or sharp 5th and are indicated using these symbols:

1st 2nd ♭3rd 4th ♯5th 6th 7th 8th

The diagrams show the ukulele fretboard in an upright position, with **high A** on the right. The **nut** (i.e. where the frets finish, just before the head) appears at the top.

The notes to be played are shown as circles, with the finger number that should be used for each note:

① = index finger	**② = middle finger**
③ = ring finger	**④ = little finger**

An **X** above the string shows that the string should **not** be played in the chord and should be **muted**, to prevent it sounding accidentally. An **O** above the string shows that it should be played as an **open** string.

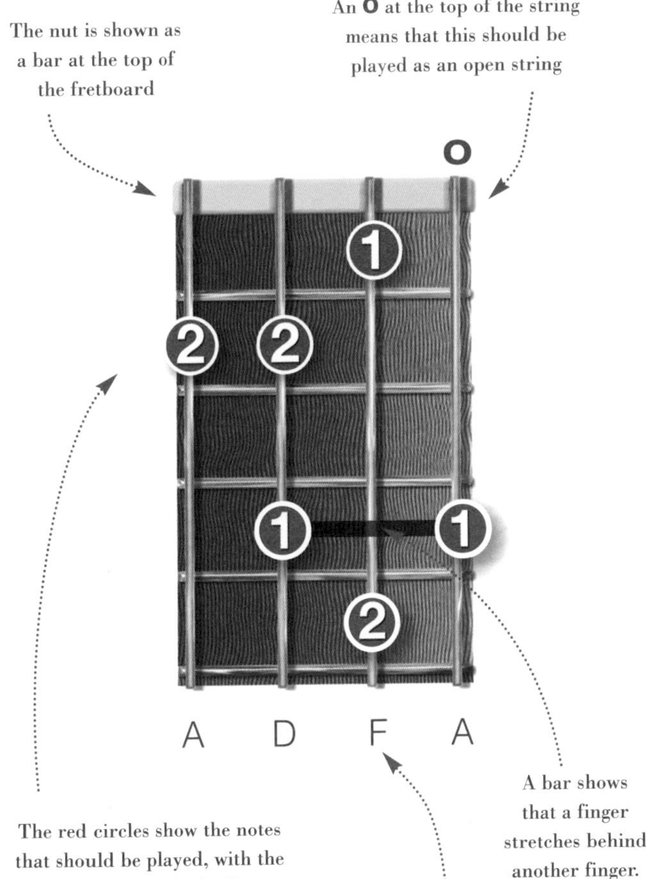
The nut is shown as a bar at the top of the fretboard
An O at the top of the string means that this should be played as an open string
O
1
2
2
1
1
2
A D F A
A bar shows that a finger stretches behind another finger.
The red circles show the notes that should be played, with the numbers relating to the fingers that should fret the notes
These are the notes that are played

Start Here
A
B♭/A#
B
C
C#/D♭
D
E♭/D#
E
F
F#/G♭
G
A♭/G#

More about the Notes

Each step on the fretboard represents a note. Each note up the fretboard is higher than the one it precedes. The difference between each note is called an **interval**, and these intervals are used to make **scales**, which in turn are used to make **chords**.

Playing every note on a piano, from left to right, using all the white and the black keys, is similar to playing every note on every string from bass to treble strings on a guitar. A standard ukulele is slightly different because although every fret represents a different interval, the standard tuning of most ukuleles presents a G string that is only two intervals lower than the top, A string. This gives the ukulele its unique high-pitched tone and means that the root note of a chord (i.e. the note that gives the chord its name) is often on the 3rd string.

This doesn't really matter when you're playing, but its essential to understand the fretboard, so here's a digram with notes up to the 5th fret.

The C on the third string is middle C on a piano.

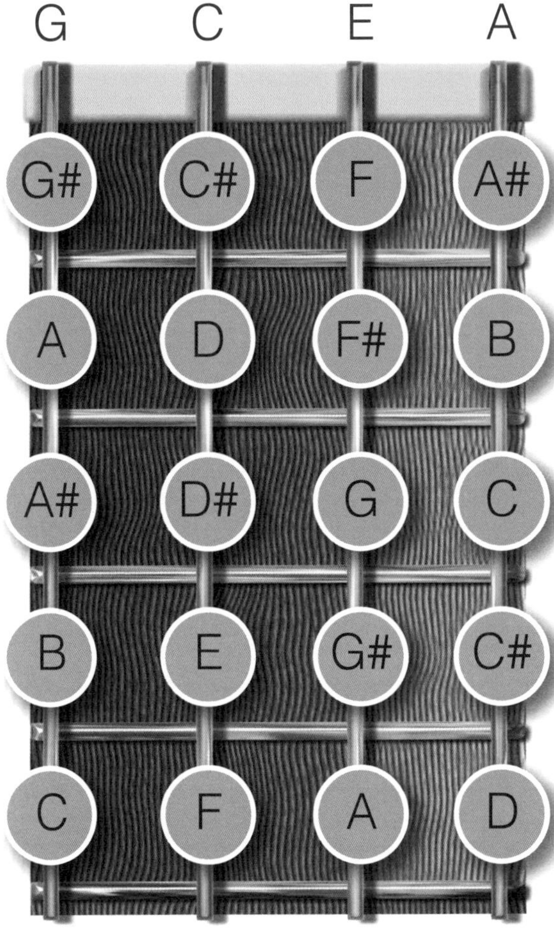

G	C	E	A
G#	C#	F	A#
A	D	F#	B
A#	D#	G	C
B	E	G#	C#
C	F	A	D

A
B♭/A♯
B
C
C♯/D♭
D
E♭/D♯
E
F
F♯/G♭
G
A♭/G♯

More about Chords, ♭ and ♯

We have tried to make the chord section as easy to use as possible, so where there is a choice of note name (e.g. F♯ or G♭) we have selected the one that you are **most likely** to come across in your playing.

The name of the note in a chord is determined by its key, so an E♯ makes the same sound as an F, in the key of C major.

Where a chord contains a flattened (♭) or sharpened (♯) interval (e.g. ♯5th), you can find the notes by playing a fret lower (for a flat) or a fret higher (for a sharp) than the interval note indicated at the top of the page.

In the keys that contain a large number of sharps or flats, **double flats** (𝄫) and **double sharps** (X) sometimes occur in the augmented and diminished chords. A **double flat** is the note **two frets** below the **named note**, while a **double sharp** is **two frets up**.

Same chord shape, different chord and names.

D°7

Diminished 7th

- This is a chord in the key of D.
- This chord requires the use of A♭ on the 4th string.
- The A♭ sounds the same as G♯, which is indicated in the fretboard diagram on page 13.

A♭°7

Diminished 7th

- This is a chord in the key of A♭.
- This chord requires the use of E𝄫 and G𝄫 on the 3rd and 2nd string.
- The E𝄫 sounds the same as the D note in the D major chord, the G𝄫 sounds the same as the F note.

Start Here
A
B♭/A#
B
C
C#/D♭
D
E♭/D#
E
F
F#/G♭
G
A♭/G#

Tuning Your Ukulele

Obviously it is critical to keep the ukulele in tune. It doesn't matter what you use, it can be a tuning fork, a pitch pipe, mobile phone app, tablet app or a keyboard.

The notes are based on specific positions on the piano:

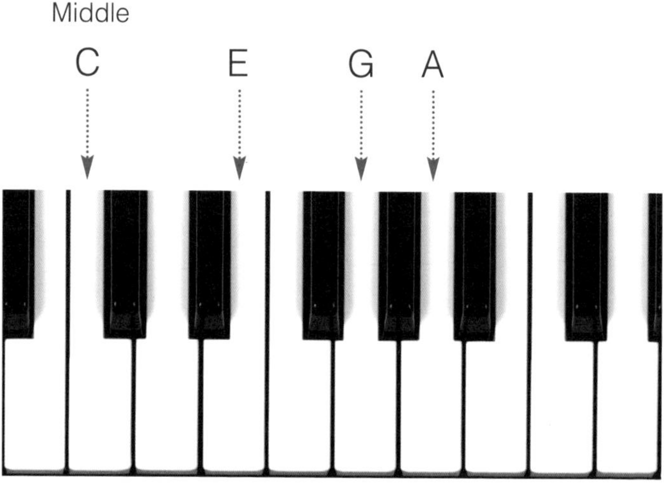

The standard tuning on a ukulele is like this:

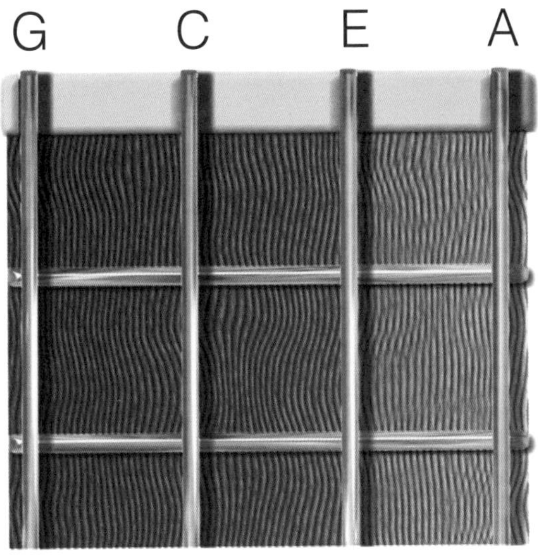

You'll see that the G on the last string is higher than the middle C on the lower string, but slightly lower than the A on the top string. It sounds more confusing than it really is; as long as you learn the chord shapes you'll be able to play with other ukulele players, and other instruments.

Start Here
A
B♭/A♯
B
C
C♯/D♭
D
E♭/D♯
E
F
F♯/G♭
G
A♭/G♯

Types of Ukulele

Soprano

Tuning

G C E A

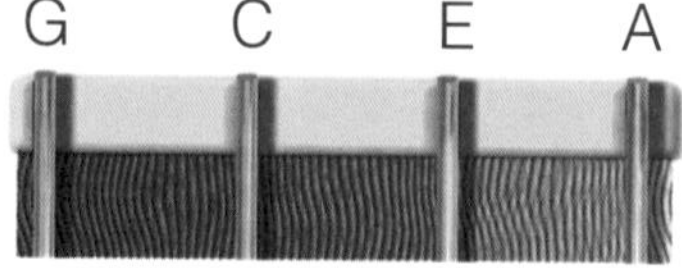

Concert

Tuning

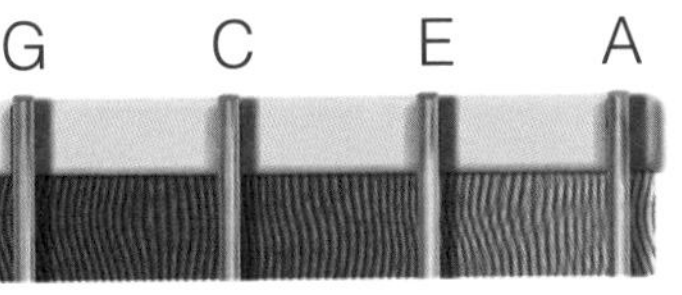

flametreemusic.com

Start Here
A
B♭/A♯
B
C
C♯/D♭
D
E♭/D♯
E
F
F♯/G♭
G
A♭/G♯

The G string on this ukulele is generally **tuned one octave lower** than the concert and soprano ukuleles.

Tenor

Tuning

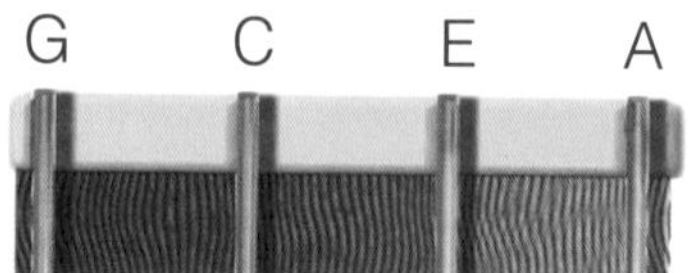

This ukulele has the same tuning as the top four strings of a guitar.

Baritone

Tuning

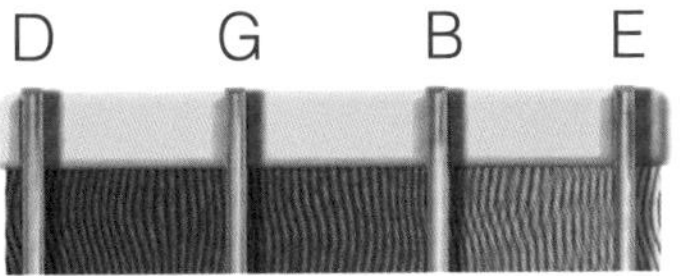

flametreemusic.com

Strumming Patterns

If you listen to a few songs you'll hear the time signatures, usually 4/4 for rock and pop, or 3/4 and 6/8 for other styles such as folk and country. Here are some simple suggestions of strumming patterns to help you get started.

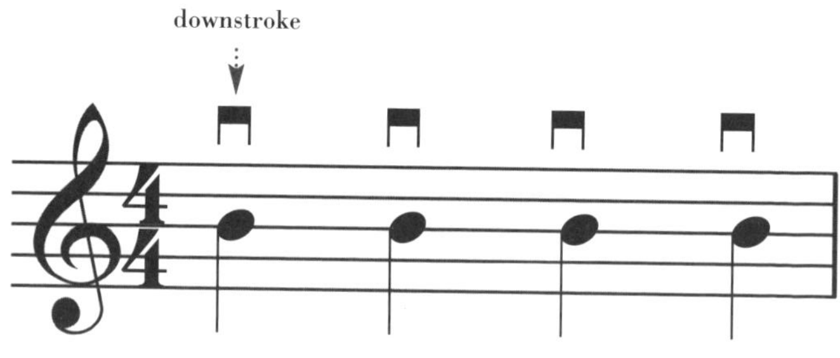

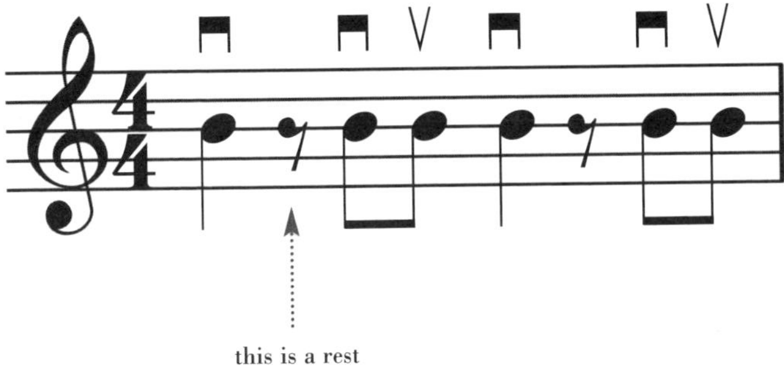

this is a rest

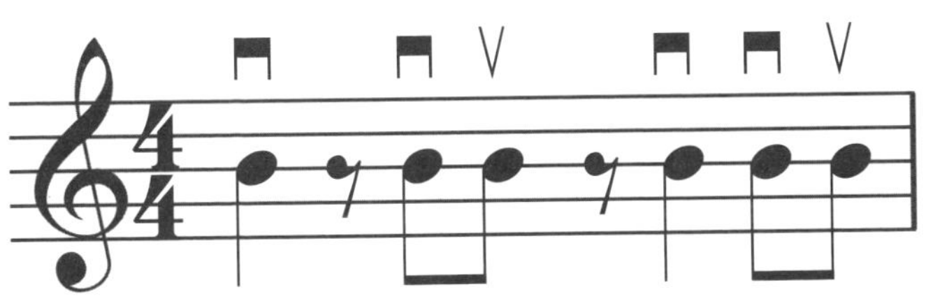

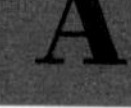

A Major

Chord Spelling

1st (A), 3rd (C♯), 5th (E)

A

Major

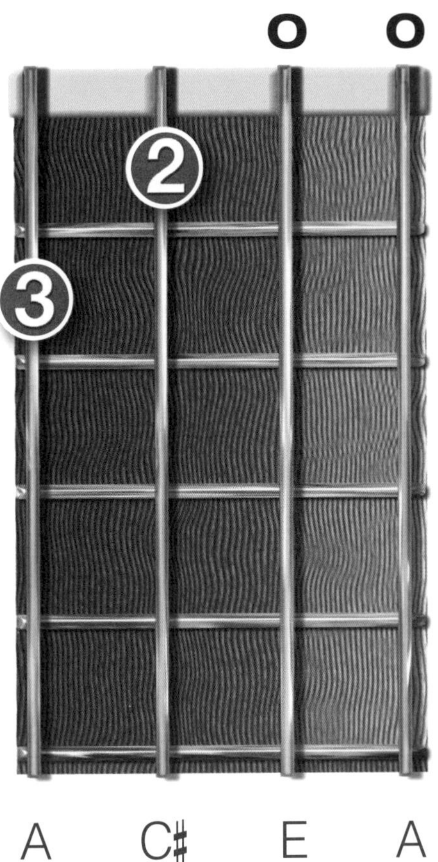

Start Here

A

B♭/A♯

B
C

C♯/D♭

D

E♭/D♯
E

F

F♯/G♭
G

A♭/G♯

Start Here
A
B♭/A♯
B
C
C♯/D♭
D
E♭/D♯
E
F
F♯/G♭
G
A♭/G♯

Am
Minor

Chord Spelling

1st (A), ♭3rd (C), 5th (E)

Am

Minor

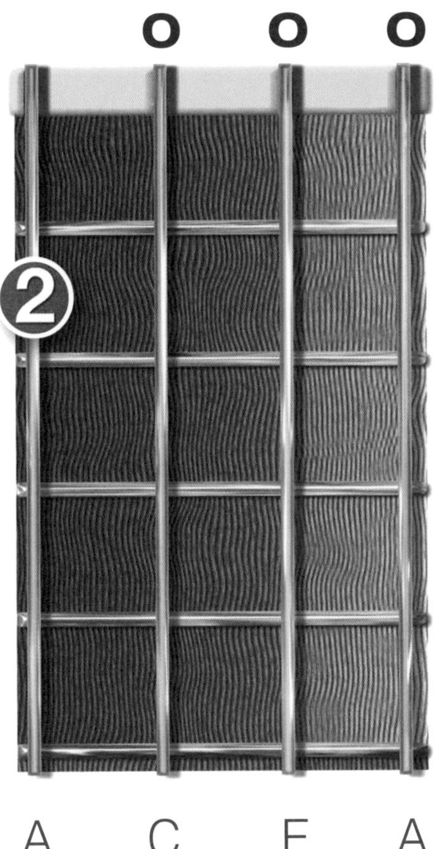

flametreemusic.com

Augmented

Chord Spelling

1st (A), 3rd (C♯), ♯5th (E♯)

Start Here

C

F

A+

Augmented

A°

Diminished

ESSENTIAL

Chord Spelling

1st (A), ♭3rd (C), ♭5th (E♭)

A°

Diminished

flametreemusic.com

A
B♭/A♯
B
C
C♯/D♭
D
E♭/D♯
E
F
F♯/G♭
G
A♭/G♯

Asus2

Suspended 2nd

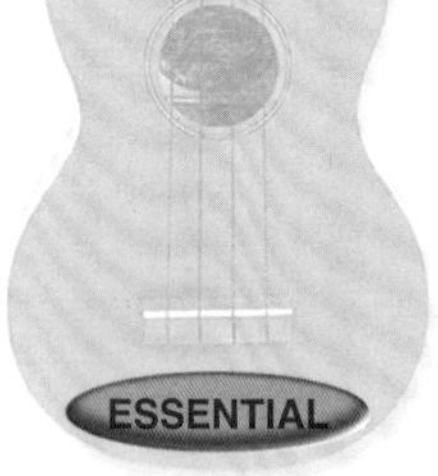

Chord Spelling

1st (A), 2nd (B), 5th (E)

Asus2

Suspended 2nd

Asus4

Suspended 4th

Chord Spelling

1st (A), 4th (D), 5th (E)

Asus4

Suspended 4th

A6

Major 6th

Chord Spelling

1st (A), 3rd (C♯), 5th (E), 6th (F♯)

A6

Major 6th

A E F♯ C♯

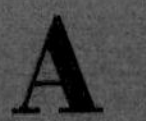

Am6

Minor 6th

Chord Spelling

1st (A), ♭3rd (C), 5th (E), 6th (F♯)

Am6

Minor 6th

flametreemusic.com

Start Here
A
B♭/A♯
B
C
C♯/D♭
D
E♭/D♯
E
F
F♯/G♭
G
A♭/G♯

A6sus4

6th Suspended 4th

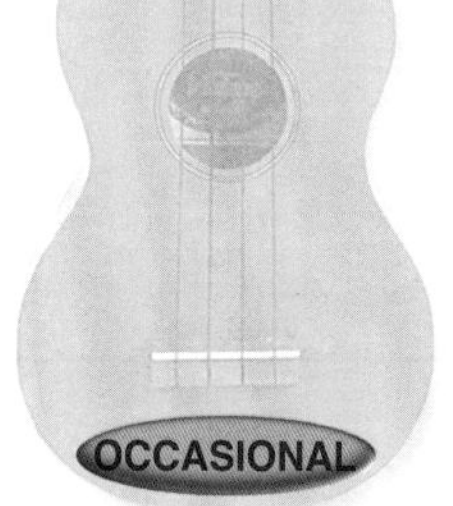

Chord Spelling

1st (A), 4th (D), 5th (E), 6th (F♯)

A6sus4

6th Suspended 4th

flametreemusic.com

Start Here

A
B♭/A♯
B
C
C♯/D♭
D
E♭/D♯
E
F
F♯/G♭
G
A♭/G♯

Amaj7

Major 7th

Chord Spelling

1st (A), 3rd (C♯), 5th (E), 7th (G♯)

Amaj7

Major 7th

Start Here
A
B♭/A♯
B
C
C♯/D♭
D
E♭/D♯
E
F
F♯/G♭
G
A♭/G♯

Am7
Minor 7th

Chord Spelling

1st (A), ♭3rd (C), 5th (E), ♭7th (G)

Am7

Minor 7th

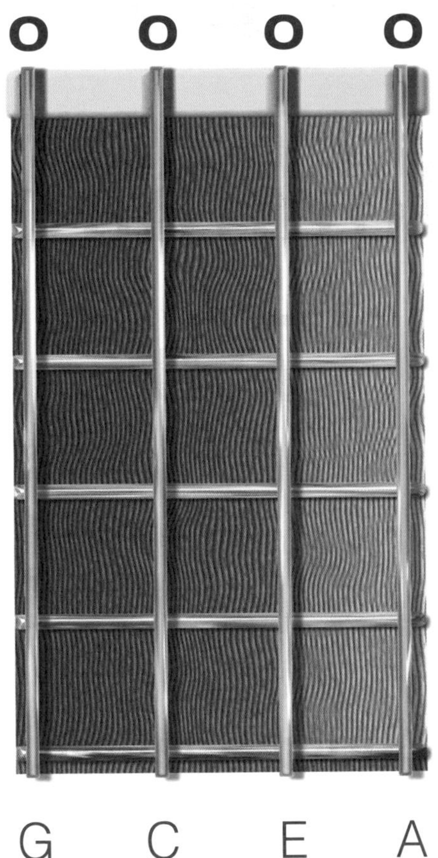

flametreemusic.com

Start Here

A
B♭/A♯
B
C
C♯/D♭
D
E♭/D♯
E
F
F♯/G♭
G
A♭/G♯

A7

Dominant 7th

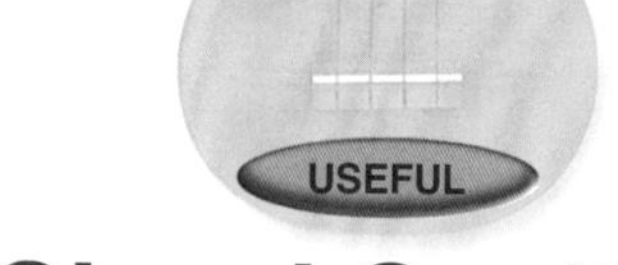

Chord Spelling

1st (A), 3rd (C♯), 5th (E), ♭7th (G)

A7

Dominant 7th

Start Here

A

B♭/A♯

B

C

C♯/D♭

D

E♭/D♯

E

F

F♯/G♭

G

A♭/G♯

A°7

Diminished 7th

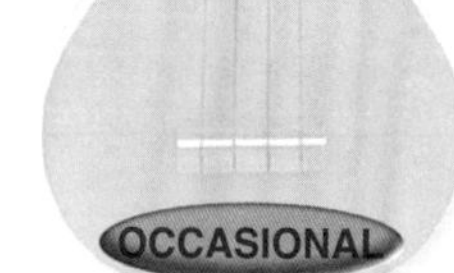

Chord Spelling

1st (A), ♭3rd (C), ♭5th (E♭), ♭♭7th (G♭

A°7

Diminished 7th

flametreemusic.com

Start Here
A
B♭/A#
B
C
C#/D♭
D
E♭/D#
E
F
F#/G♭
G
A♭/G#

A7sus4

Dominant 7th Suspended 4th

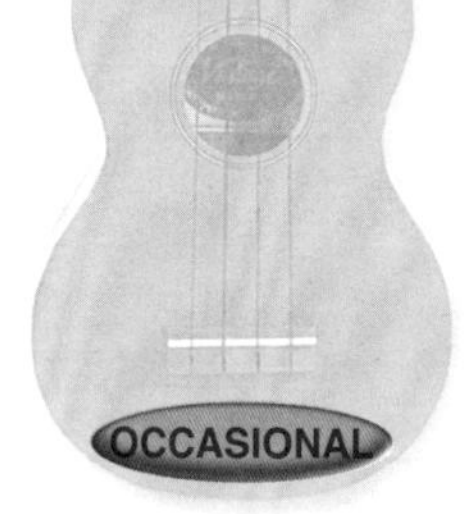

Chord Spelling

1st (A), 4th (D), 5th (E), ♭7th (G)

A7sus4

Dominant 7th Suspended 4th

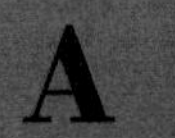

A/9

Major add 9th

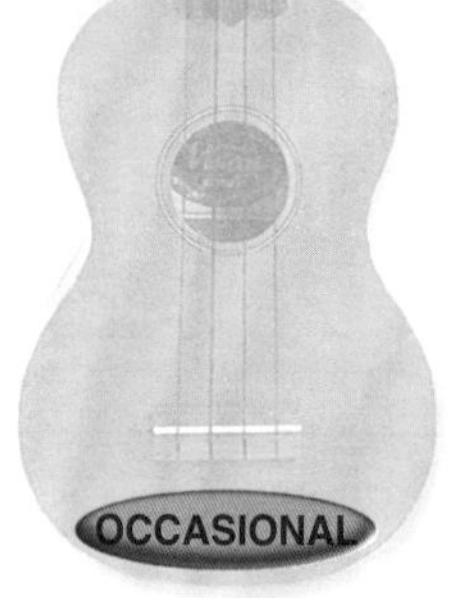

Chord Spelling

1st (A), 3rd (C♯), 5th (E), 9th (B)

A/9

Major add 9th

A C♯ E B

flamestreemusic.com

Start Here
A
B♭/A♯
B
C
C♯/D♭
D
E♭/D♯
E
F
F♯/G♭
G
A♭/G♯

B♭ Major

Chord Spelling

1st (B♭), 3rd (D), 5th (F)

B♭

Major

B♭ D F B♭

flametreemusic.com

B♭m

Minor

Chord Spelling

1st (B♭), ♭3rd (D♭), 5th (F)

B♭m

Minor

B♭ D♭ F B♭

B♭+ Augmented

Chord Spelling

1st (B♭), 3rd (D), ♯5th (F♯)

B♭+

Augmented

B♭ D F♯ B♭

flametreemusic.com

Start Here
A
B♭/A♯
B
C
C♯/D♭
D
E♭/D♯
E
F
F♯/G♭
G
A♭/G♯

Diminished

Chord Spelling

1st (B♭), ♭3rd (D♭), ♭5th (F♭)

B♭°

Diminished

Start Here
A
B♭/A#
B
C
C#/D♭
D
E♭/D#
E
F
F#/G♭
G
A♭/G#

B♭sus2

Suspended 2nd

Chord Spelling

1st (B♭), 2nd (C), 5th (F)

B♭sus2

Suspended 2nd

Start Here
A
B♭/A♯
B
C
C♯/D♭
D
E♭/D♯
E
F
F♯/G♭
G
A♭/G♯

B♭sus4

Suspended 4th

Chord Spelling

1st (B♭), 4th (E♭), 5th (F)

B♭sus4

Suspended 4th

B♭ E♭ F B♭

flametreemusic.com

B♭6

Major 6th

Chord Spelling

1st (B♭), 3rd (D), 5th (F), 6th (G)

B♭6

Major 6th

flametreemusic.com

Start Here

A

B♭/A♯

B

C

C♯/D♭

D

E♭/D♯

E

F

F♯/G♭

G

A♭/G♯

B♭m6

Minor 6th

Chord Spelling

1st (B♭), ♭3rd (D♭), 5th (F), 6th (G

B♭m6

Minor 6th

G D♭ F B♭

B♭6sus4

6th Suspended 4th

Chord Spelling

1st (B♭), 4th (E♭), 5th (F), 6th (G)

B♭6sus4

6th Suspended 4th

flametreemusic.com

B♭maj7

Major 7th

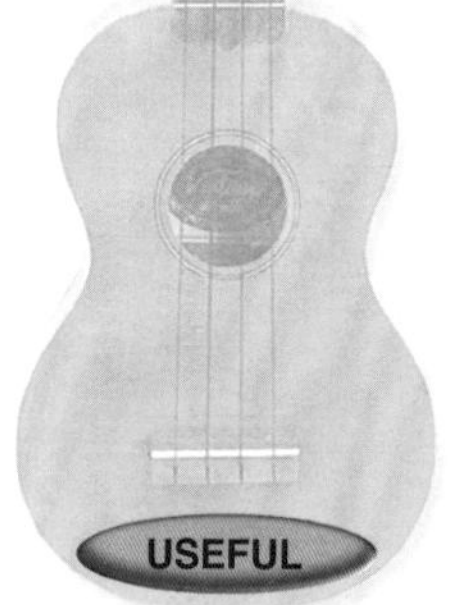

USEFUL

Chord Spelling

1st (B♭), 3rd (D), 5th (F), 7th (A)

B♭maj7

Major 7th

A D F B♭

flametreemusic.com

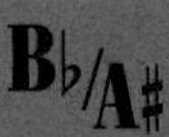

B♭m7

Minor 7th

Chord Spelling

1st (B♭), ♭3rd (D♭), 5th (F), ♭7th (A♭)

B♭m7

Minor 7th

flametreemusic.com

B♭7 Dominant 7th

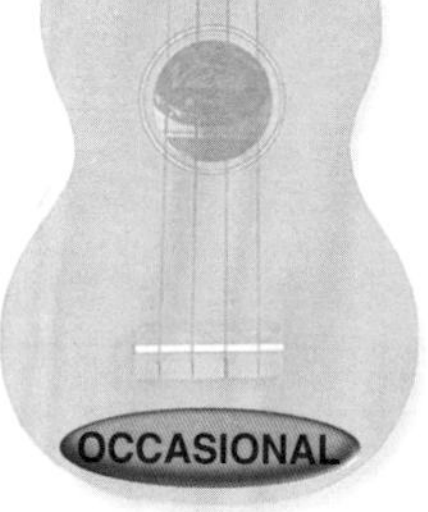

Chord Spelling

1st (B♭), 3rd (D), 5th (F), ♭7th (A♭)

B♭7

Dominant 7th

A♭ D F B♭

flametreemusic.com

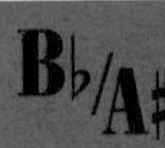

B♭°7

Diminished 7th

Chord Spelling

1st (B♭), ♭3rd (D♭), ♭5th (F♭), ♭♭7th (A♭♭)

B♭°7

Diminished 7th

Start Here
A
B♭/A♯
B
C
C♯/D♭
D
E♭/D♯
E
F
F♯/G♭
G
A♭/G♯

B♭7sus4

Dominant 7th Suspended 4th

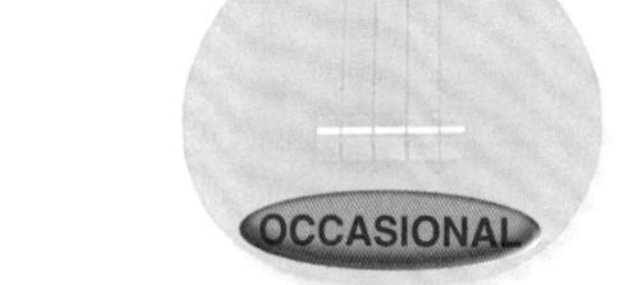

Chord Spelling

1st (B♭), 4th (E♭), 5th (F), ♭7th (A♭)

B♭7sus4

Dominant 7th Suspended 4th

A♭ E♭ F B♭

flametreemusic.com

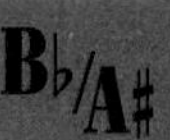

A♭/G♯

Start Here
A
B♭/A♯
B
C
C♯/D♭
D
E♭/D♯
E
F
F♯/G♭
G
A♭/G♯

B♭/9

Major add 9th

Chord Spelling

1st (B♭), 3rd (D), 5th (F), 9th (C)

B♭/9

Major add 9th

flametreemusic.com

B♭/A#
B
C
C#/D♭
D
E♭/D#
E
F
F#/G♭
G
A♭/G#

B Major

Chord Spelling

1st (B), 3rd (D♯), 5th (F♯)

B

Major

B D♯ F♯ B

flametreemusic.com

Bm
Minor

Chord Spelling

1st (B), ♭3rd (D), 5th (F♯)

Bm

Minor

B+

Augmented

Chord Spelling

1st (B), 3rd (D♯), ♯5th (Fx)

B+

Augmented

B°

Diminished

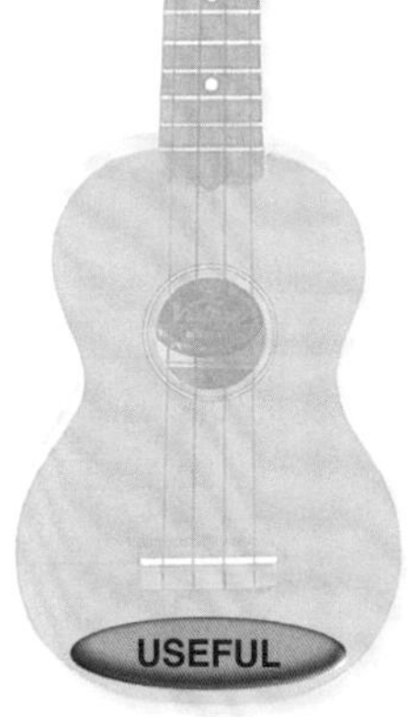

Chord Spelling

1st (B), ♭3rd (D), ♭5th (F)

B°

Diminished

B D F B

flametreemusic.com

Bsus2

Suspended 2nd

Chord Spelling

1st (B), 2nd (C♯), 5th (F♯)

Bsus2

Suspended 2nd

flametreemusic.com

Bsus4

Suspended 4th

Chord Spelling

1st (B), 4th (E), 5th (F♯)

Bsus4

Suspended 4th

B6

Major 6th

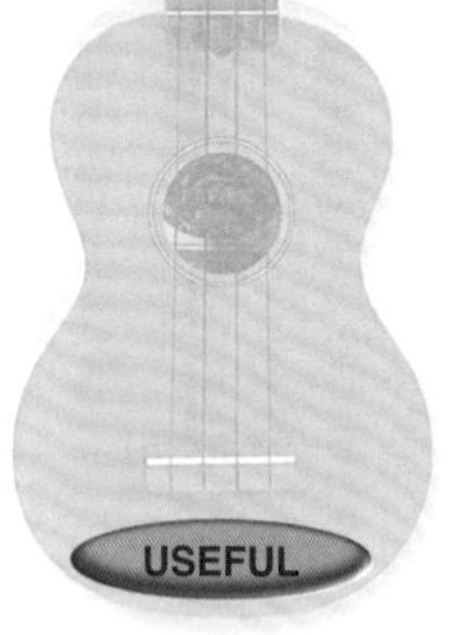

Chord Spelling

1st (B), 3rd (D♯), 5th (F♯), 6th (G♯)

B6

Major 6th

G♯ D♯ F♯ B

flametreemusic.com

Start Here
A
B♭/A♯
B
C
C♯/D♭
D
E♭/D♯
E
F
F♯/G♭
G
A♭/G♯

Bm6

Minor 6th

Chord Spelling

1st (B), ♭3rd (D), 5th (F♯), 6th (G♯)

Bm6

Minor 6th

Start Here
A
B♭/A#
B
C
C#/D♭
D
E♭/D#
E
F
F#/G♭
G
A♭/G#

B6sus4

6th Suspended 4th

Chord Spelling

1st (B), 4th (E), 5th (F#), 6th (G#)

B6sus4

6th Suspended 4th

Bmaj7

Major 7th

Chord Spelling

1st (B), 3rd (D♯), 5th (F♯), 7th (A♯)

Bmaj7

Major 7th

Start Here
A
B♭/A♯
B
C
C♯/D♭
D
E♭/D♯
E
F
F♯/G♭
G
A♭/G♯

Start Here
A
B♭/A♯
B
C
C♯/D♭
D
E♭/D♯
E
F
F♯/G♭
G
A♭/G♯

Bm7

Minor 7th

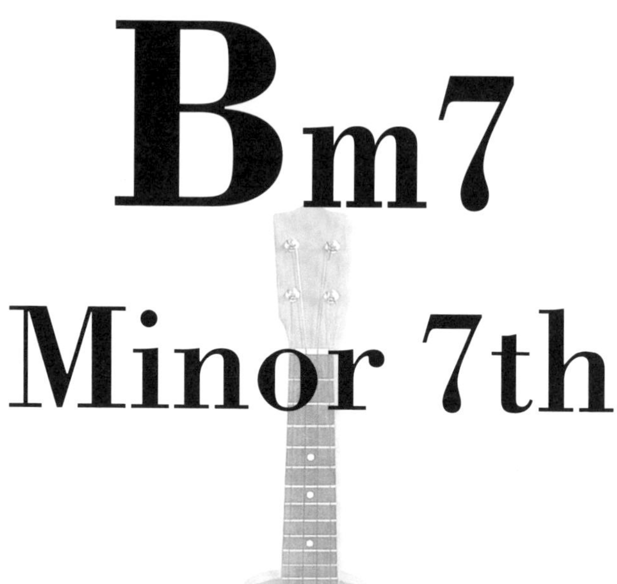

Chord Spelling

1st (B), ♭3rd (D), 5th (F♯), ♭7th (A)

Bm7

Minor 7th

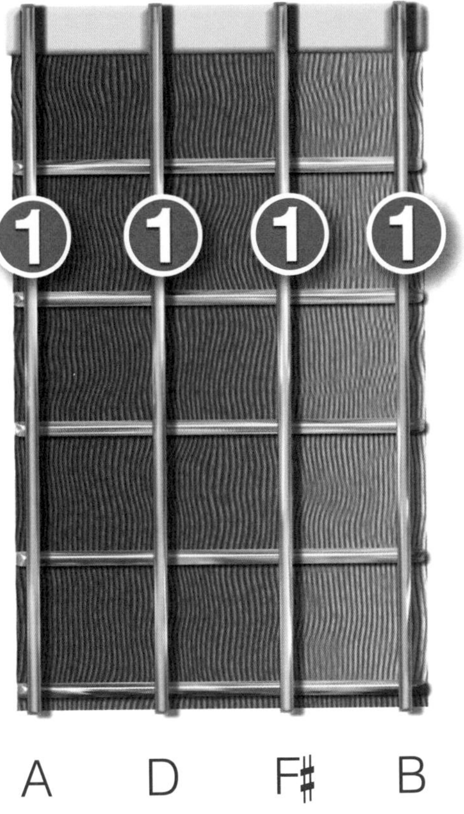

B7

Dominant 7th

USEFUL

Chord Spelling

1st (B), 3rd (D♯), 5th (F♯), ♭7th (A)

B7

Dominant 7th

A D♯ F♯ B

flametreemusic.com

B°7

Diminished 7th

OCCASIONAL

Chord Spelling

1st (B), ♭3rd (D), ♭5th (F), 𝄫7th (A♭)

B°7

Diminished 7th

A♭ D F B

flametreemusic.com

B7sus4

Dominant 7th Suspended 4th

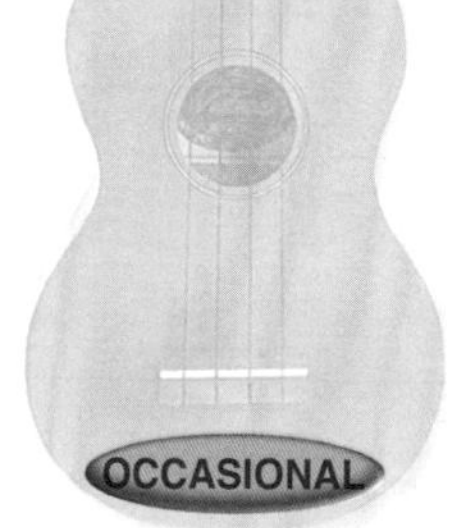

Chord Spelling

1st (B), 4th (E), 5th (F♯), ♭7th (A)

B7sus4

Dominant 7th Suspended 4th

B/9

Major add 9th

Chord Spelling

1st (B), 3rd (D♯), 5th (F♯), 9th (C♯)

B/9

Major add 9th

B D♯ F♯ C♯

flametreemusic.com

C Major

ESSENTIAL

Chord Spelling

1st (C), 3rd (E), 5th (G)

C

Major

Cm

Minor

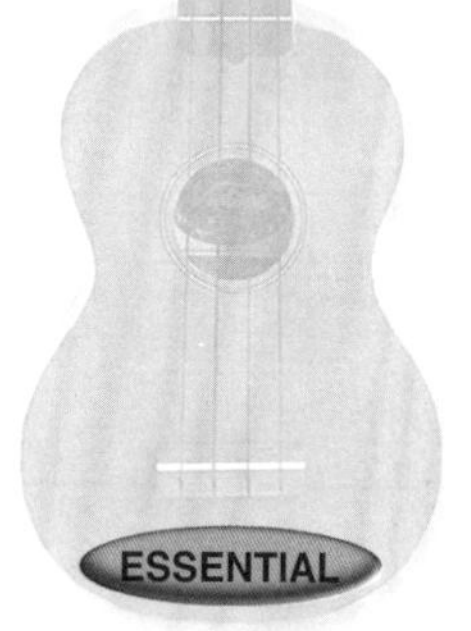

Chord Spelling

1st (C), ♭3rd (E♭), 5th (G)

Cm

Minor

C+

Augmented

Chord Spelling

1st (C), 3rd (E), ♯5th (G♯)

C+

Augmented

flametreemusic.com

C°

Diminished

Chord Spelling

1st (C), ♭3rd (E♭), ♭5th (G♭)

C°

Diminished

E♭ G♭ C

flametreemusic.com

Csus2

Suspended 2nd

Chord Spelling

1st (C), 2nd (D), 5th (G)

Csus2

Suspended 2nd

Csus4

Suspended 4th

USEFUL

Chord Spelling

1st (C), 4th (F), 5th (G)

Csus4

Suspended 4th

Start Here
A
B♭/A♯
B
C
C♯/D♭
D
E♭/D♯
E
F
F♯/G♭
G
A♭/G♯

C6

Major 6th

Chord Spelling

1st (C), 3rd (E), 5th (G), 6th (A)

C6

Major 6th

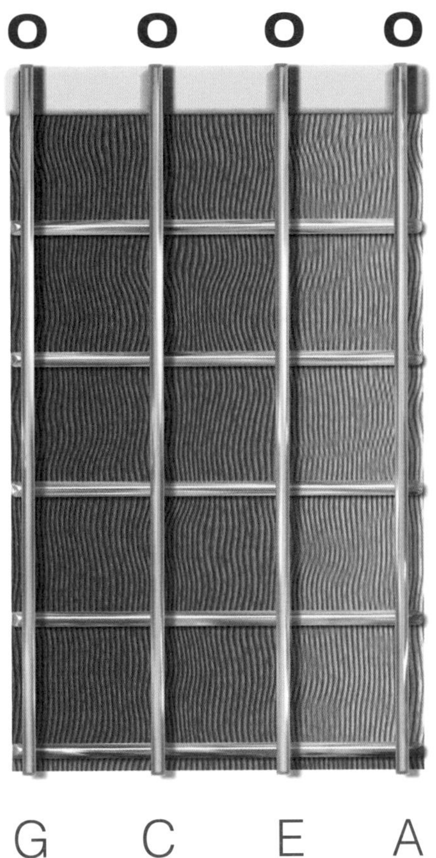
o o o o
G C E A

Start Here
A
B♭/A♯
B
C

C♯/D♭
D

E♭/D♯
E
F

G
A♭/G♯

Cm6

Minor 6th

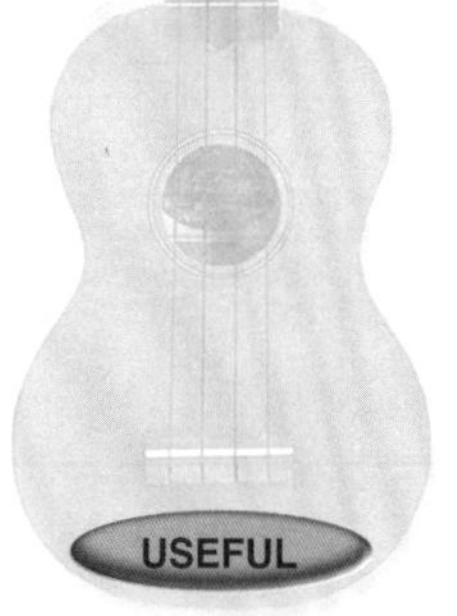

Chord Spelling

1st (C), ♭3rd (E♭), 5th (G), 6th (A)

Cm6

Minor 6th

C6sus4

6th Suspended 4th

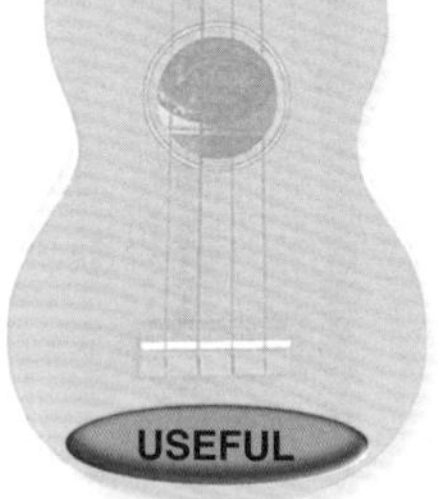

Chord Spelling

1st (C), 4th (F), 5th (G), 6th (A)

C6sus4

6th Suspended 4th

flametreemusic.com

A
B♭/A♯
B
C
C♯/D♭
D
E♭/D♯
E
F
F♯/G♭
G
A♭/G♯

Cmaj7

Major 7th

Chord Spelling

1st (C), 3rd (E), 5th (G), 7th (B)

Cmaj7

Major 7th

flametreemusic.com

Start Here
A
B♭/A#
B
C
C#/D♭
D
E♭/D#
E
F
F#/G♭
G
A♭/G#

Cm7

Minor 7th

Chord Spelling

1st (C), ♭3rd (E♭), 5th (G), ♭7th (B♭)

Cm7

Minor 7th

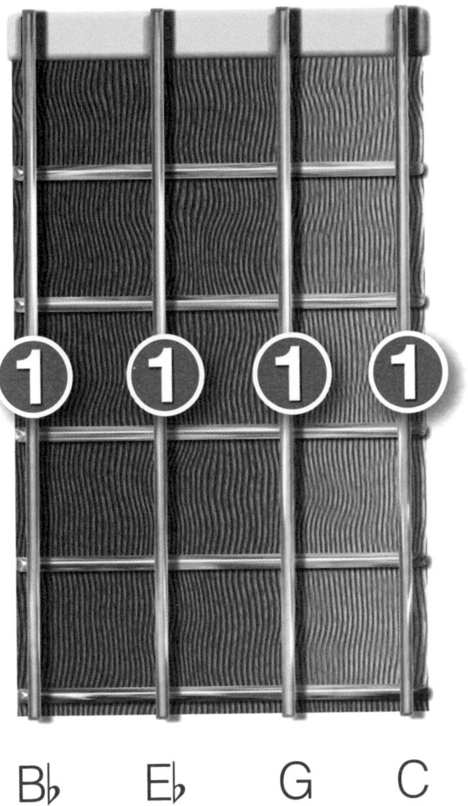

B♭ E♭ G C

flametreemusic.com

Start Here
A
B♭/A♯
B
C
C♯/D♭
D
E♭/D♯
E
F
F♯/G♭
G
A♭/G♯

C7 Dominant 7th

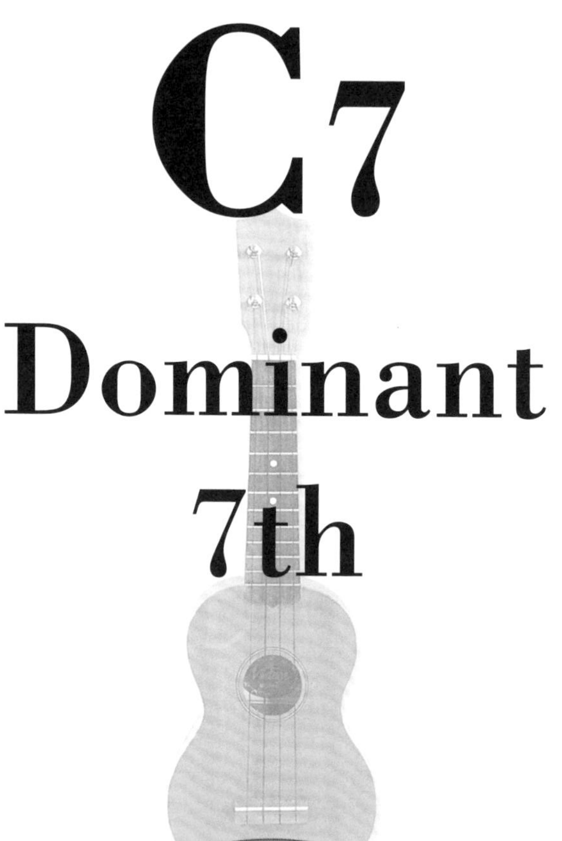

Chord Spelling

1st (C), 3rd (E), 5th (G), ♭7th (B♭)

C7

Dominant 7th

Start Here
A
B♭/A♯
B
C
C♯/D♭
D
E♭/D♯
E
F
F♯/G♭
G
A♭/G♯

C°7

Diminished 7th

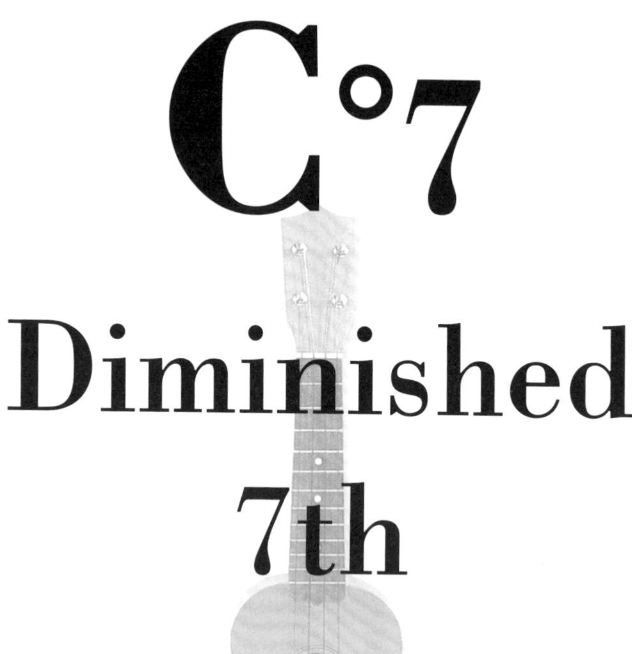

Chord Spelling

1st (C), ♭3rd (E♭), ♭5th (G♭), ♭♭7th (B♭♭)

C°7

Diminished 7th

Start Here
A
B♭/A♯
B
C
C♯/D♭
D
E♭/D♯
E
F
F♯/G♭
G
A♭/G♯

Start Here
A
B♭/A#
B
C
C#/D♭
D
E♭/D#
E
F
F#/G♭
G
A♭/G#

C7sus4

Dominant 7th Suspended 4th

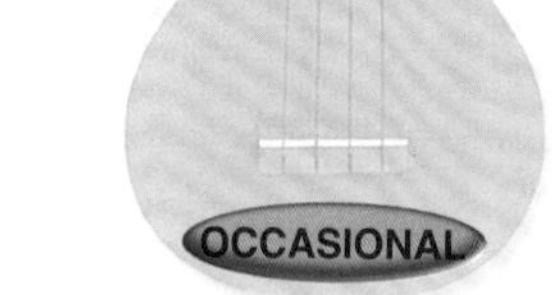

Chord Spelling

1st (C), 4th (F), 5th (G), ♭7th (B♭)

C7sus4

Dominated 7th Suspended 4th

flametreemusic.com

C/9

Major add 9th

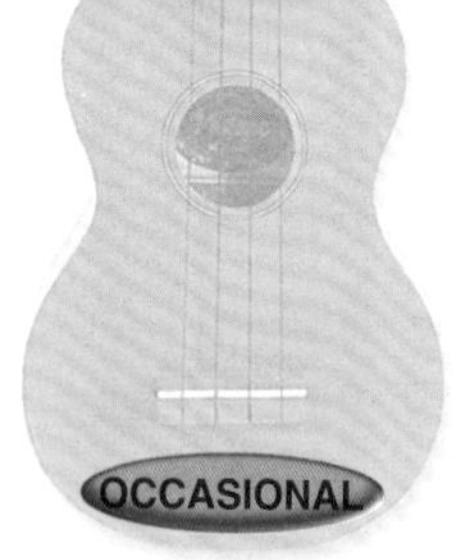

Chord Spelling

1st (C), 3rd (E), 5th (G), 9th (D)

C/9

Major add 9th

flametreemusic.com

Chord Spelling

1st (C♯), 3rd (E♯), 5th (G♯)

C♯

Major

C♯m

Minor

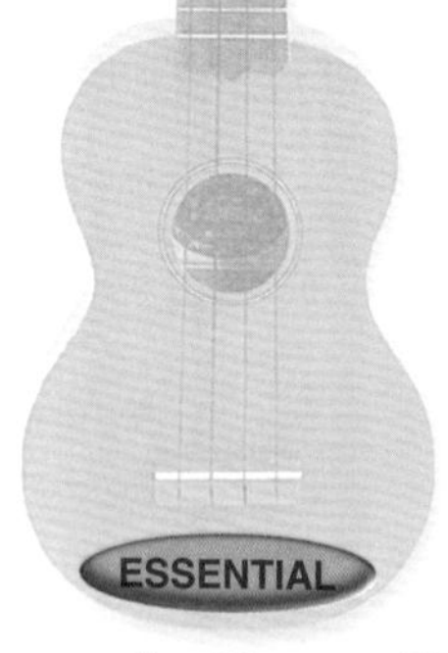

Chord Spelling

1st (C♯), ♭3rd (E), 5th (G♯)

C♯m

Minor

G♯ C♯ E C♯

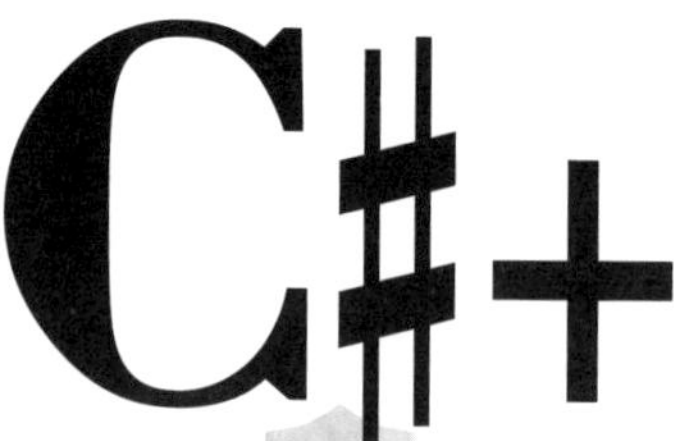

C♯+ Augmented

Chord Spelling

1st (C♯), 3rd (E♯), ♯5th (Gx)

C♯+

Augmented

Start Here
A
B♭/A♯
B
C
C♯/D♭
D
E♭/D♯
E
F
F♯/G♭
G
A♭/G♯

Start Here
A
B♭/A♯
B
C
C♯/D♭
D
E♭/D♯
E
F
F♯/G♭
G
A♭/G♯

C♯°

Diminished

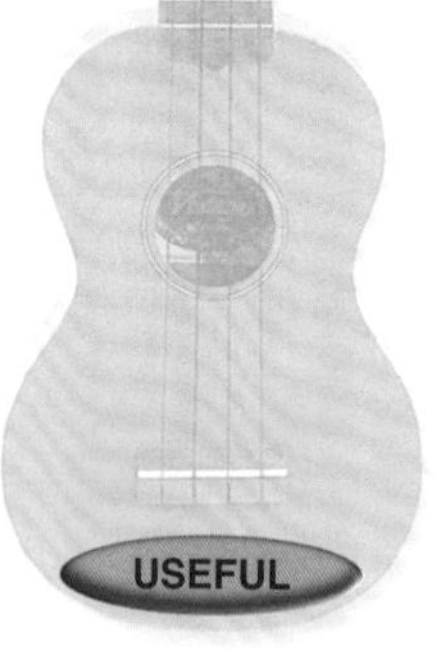

Chord Spelling

1st (C♯), ♭3rd (E), ♭5th (G)

C♯°

Diminished

C♯sus2

Suspended 2nd

Chord Spelling

1st (C♯), 2nd (D♯), 5th (G♯)

C♯sus2

Suspended 2nd

flametreemusic.com

C♯sus4

Suspended 4th

Chord Spelling

1st (C♯), 4th (F♯), 5th (G♯)

C♯sus4

Suspended 4th

G♯ C♯ F♯ C♯

Start Here
A
B♭/A♯
B
C
C♯/D♭
D
E♭/D♯
E
F
F♯/G♭
G
A♭/G♯

Start Here
A
B♭/A♯
B
C
C♯/D♭
D
E♭/D♯
E
F
F♯/G♭
G
A♭/G♯

C♯6

Major 6th

USEFUL

Chord Spelling

1st (C♯), 3rd (E♯), 5th (G♯), 6th (A♯)

C♯6

Major 6th

G♯ C♯ E♯ A♯

C♯m6

Minor 6th

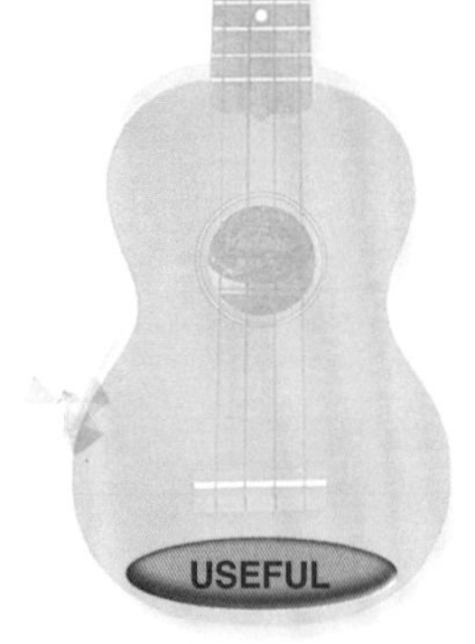

Chord Spelling

1st (C♯), ♭3rd (E), 5th (G♯), 6th (A♯)

C♯m6

Minor 6th

Start Here

A

B♭/A♯

B

C

C♯/D♭

D

E♭/D♯

E

F

F♯/G♭

G

A♭/G♯

C♯6sus4

6th Suspended 4th

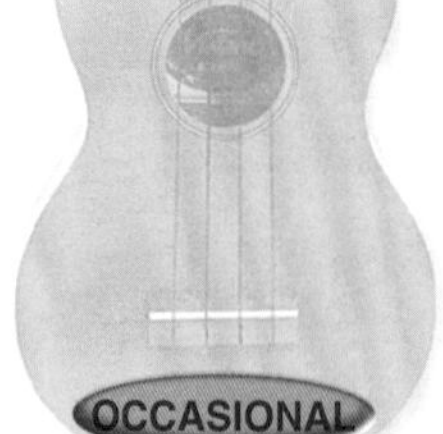

Chord Spelling

1st (C♯), 4th (F♯), 5th (G♯), 6th (A♯)

C♯6sus4

6th Suspended 4th

G♯ C♯ F♯ A♯

flametreemusic.com

Start Here
A
B♭/A♯
B
C
C♯/D♭
D
E♭/D♯
E
F
F♯/G♭
G
A♭/G♯

Chord Spelling

1st (C♯), 3rd (E♯), 5th (G♯), 7th (B♯)

C♯maj7

Major 7th

Start Here
A
B♭/A♯
B
C
C♯/D♭
D
E♭/D♯
E
F
F♯/G♭
G
A♭/G♯

Start Here
A
B♭/A♯
B
C
C♯/D♭
D
E♭/D♯
E
F
F♯/G♭
G
A♭/G♯

C♯m7

Minor 7th

Chord Spelling

1st (C♯), ♭3rd (E), 5th (G♯), ♭7th (B

C♯m7

Minor 7th

C♯7

Dominant 7th

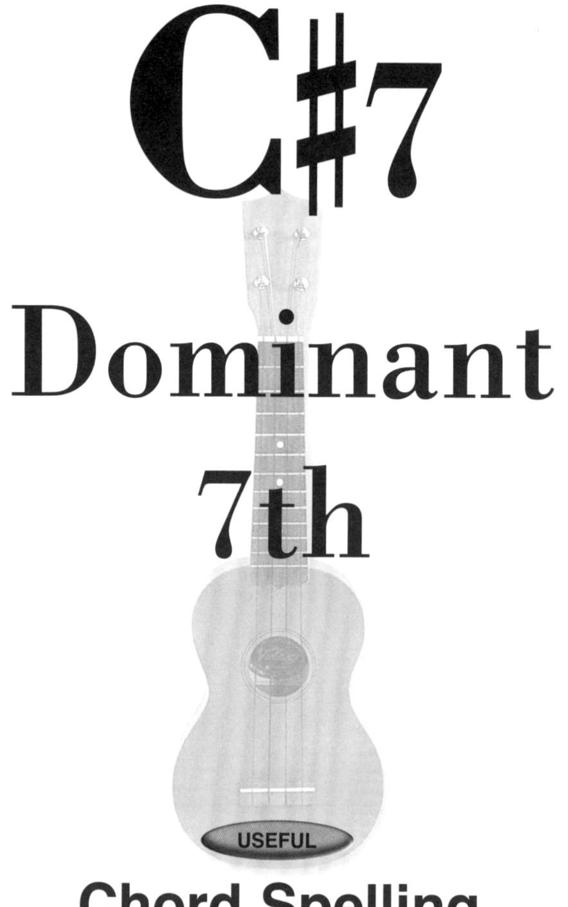

Chord Spelling

1st (C♯), 3rd (E♯), 5th (G♯), ♭7th (B)

C♯7

Dominant 7th

Start Here
A
B♭/A♯
B
C
C♯/D♭
D
E♭/D♯
E
F
F♯/G♭
G
A♭/G♯

C♯°7 Diminished 7th

USEFUL

Chord Spelling

1st (C♯), ♭3rd (E), ♭5th (G), 𝄫7th (B♭)

C♯°7

Diminished 7th

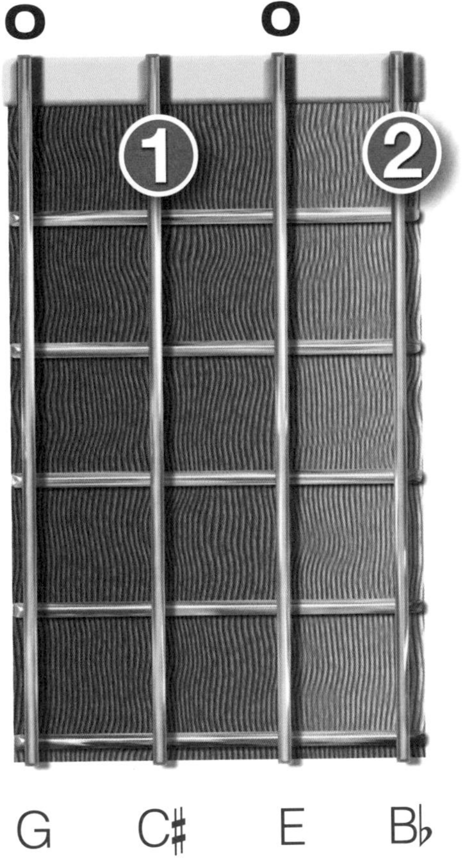

G C♯ E B♭

flametreemusic.com

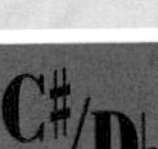

C♯7sus4

Dominant 7th Suspended 4th

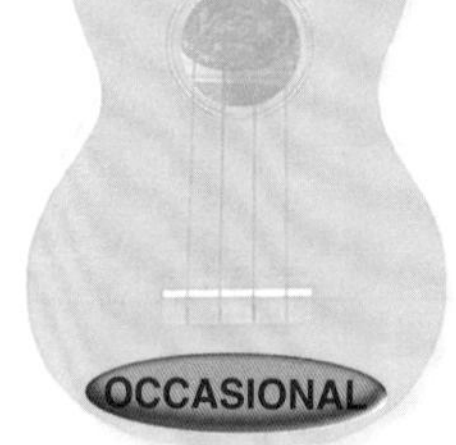

Chord Spelling

1st (C♯), 4th (F♯), 5th (G♯), ♭7th (B)

C♯7sus4

Dominant 7th Suspended 4th

G♯ C♯ F♯ B

Start Here

A

B♭/A♯

B

C
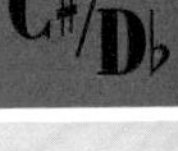
C♯/D♭
D

E♭/D♯

E

F

F♯/G♭

G
A♭/G♯

C♯/9

Major add 9th

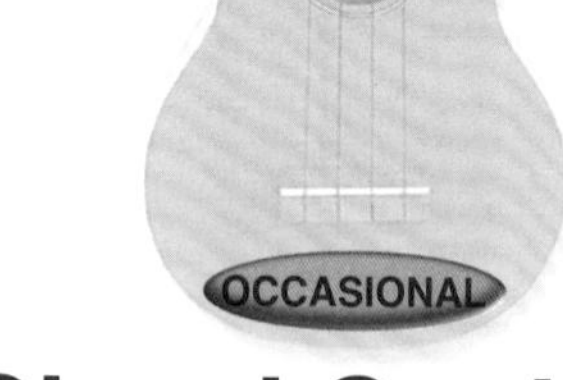

Chord Spelling

1st (C♯), 3rd (E♯), 5th (G♯), 9th (D♯)

C♯/9

Major add 9th

G♯ D♯ E♯ C♯

flametreemusic.com

Start Here
A
B♭/A♯
B
C
C♯/D♭
D
E♭/D♯
E
F
F♯/G♭
G
A♭/G♯

Start Here
A
B♭/A♯
B
C
C♯/D♭
D
E♭/D♯
E
F
F♯/G♭
G
A♭/G♯

D Major

Chord Spelling

1st (D), 3rd (F♯), 5th (A)

D

Major

Dm

Minor

ESSENTIAL

Chord Spelling

1st (D), ♭3rd (F), 5th (A)

Dm

Minor

flametreemusic.com

D+

Augmented

USEFUL

Chord Spelling

1st (D), 3rd (F♯), ♯5th (A♯)

D+

Augmented

flametreemusic.com

Start Here
A
B♭/A♯
B
C
C♯/D♭
D
E♭/D♯
E
F
F♯/G♭
G
A♭/G♯

Start Here
A
B♭/A♯
B
C
C♯/D♭
D
E♭/D♯
E
F
F♯/G♭
G
A♭/G♯

D°

Diminished

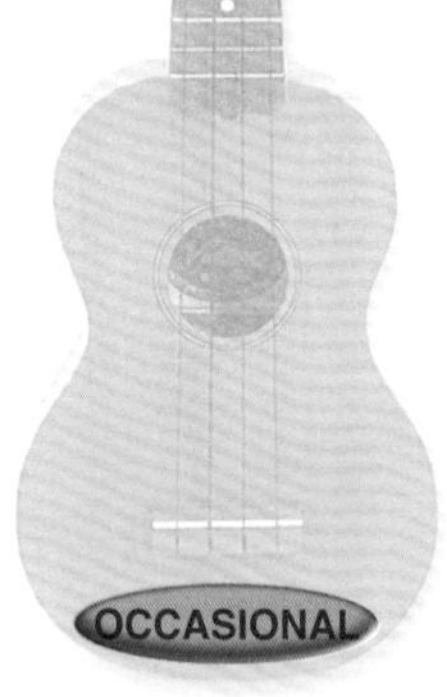

Chord Spelling

1st (D), ♭3rd (F), ♭5th (A♭)

D°

Diminished

flametreemusic.com

Start Here

E♭/D♯

Start Here
A
B♭/A♯
B
C
C♯/D♭
D
E♭/D♯
E
F
F♯/G♭
G
A♭/G♯

Dsus2

Suspended 2nd

Chord Spelling

1st (D), 2nd (E), 5th (A)

Dsus2

Suspended 2nd

Dsus4

Suspended 4th

Chord Spelling

1st (D), 4th (G), 5th (A)

Dsus4

Suspended 4th

flamtreemusic.com

D6

Major 6th

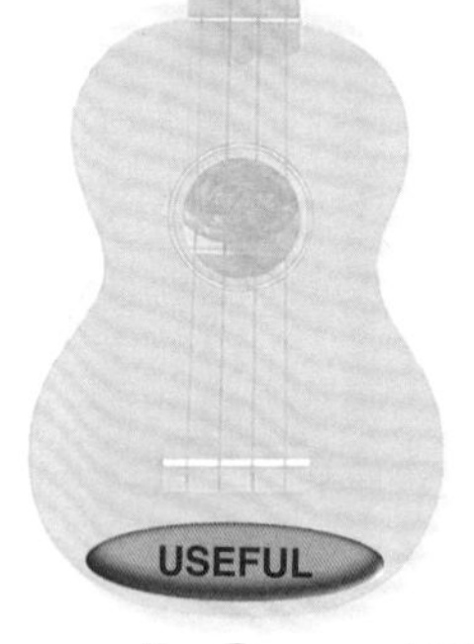

Chord Spelling

1st (D), 3rd (F♯), 5th (A), 6th (B)

D6

Major 6th

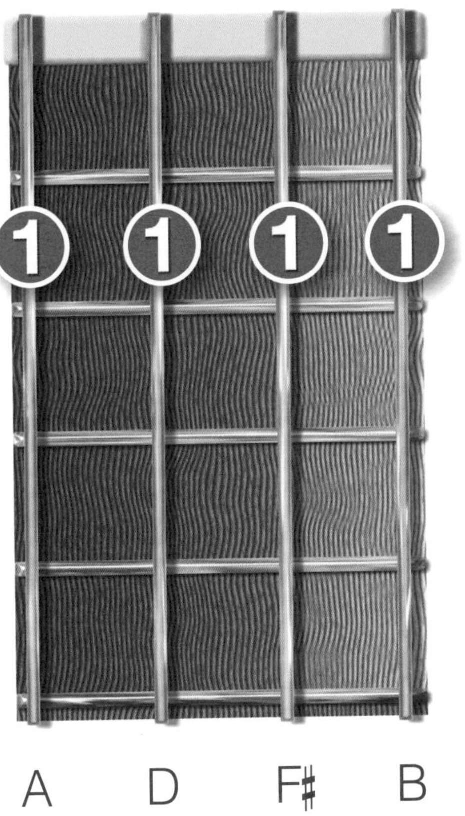

Dm6

Minor 6th

Chord Spelling

1st (D), ♭3rd (F), 5th (A), 6th (B)

Dm6

Minor 6th

flametreemusic.com

D6sus4

6th Suspended 4th

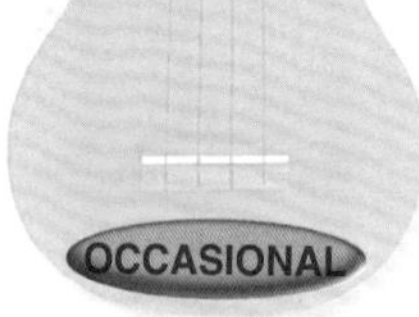

Chord Spelling

1st (D), 4th (G), 5th (A), 6th (B)

D6sus4

6th Suspended 4th

A D G B

Start Here
A
B♭/A♯
B
C
C♯/D♭
D
E♭/D♯
E
F
F♯/G♭
G
A♭/G♯

Dmaj7

Major 7th

Chord Spelling

1st (D), 3rd (F♯), 5th (A), 7th (C♯)

Dmaj7

Major 7th

A D F♯ C♯

flametreemusic.com

Start Here
A
B♭/A♯
B
C
C♯/D♭
D
E♭/D♯
E
F
F♯/G♭
G
A♭/G♯

Dm7
Minor 7th

USEFUL

Chord Spelling

1st (D), ♭3rd (F), 5th (A), ♭7th (C)

Dm7

Minor 7th

flametreemusic.com

Start Here

A

B♭/A♯

B

C

C♯/D♭

D

E♭/D♯

E

F

F♯/G♭

G

A♭/G♯

D7

Dominant 7th

USEFUL

Chord Spelling

1st (D), 3rd (F♯), 5th (A), ♭7th (C)

Start Here
A
B♭/A♯
B
C
C♯/D♭
D
E♭/D♯
E
F
F♯/G♭
G
A♭/G♯

D7

Dominant 7th

D°7

Diminished 7th

Chord Spelling

1st (D), ♭3rd (F), ♭5th (A♭), ♭♭7th (C♭

D°7

Diminished 7th

D7sus4

Dominant 7th Suspended 4th

Chord Spelling

1st (D), 4th (G), 5th (A), ♭7th (C)

D7sus4

Dominant 7th Suspended 4th

flametreemusic.com

A
B♭/A#
B
C
C#/D♭
D
E♭/D#
E
F
F#/G♭
G
A♭/G#

D/9

Major add 9th

Chord Spelling

1st (D), 3rd (F♯), 5th (A), 9th (E)

D/9

Major add 9th

A E F♯ D

flametreemusic.com

Start Here
A
B♭/A♯
B
C
C♯/D♭
D
E♭/D♯
E
F
F♯/G♭
G
A♭/G♯

E♭ Major

Chord Spelling

1st (E♭), 3rd (G), 5th (B♭)

E♭

Major

flametreemusic.com

E♭m
Minor

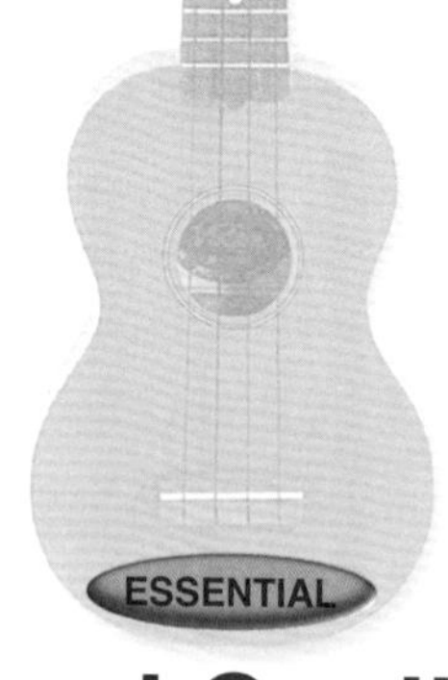

Chord Spelling

1st (E♭), ♭3rd (G♭), 5th (B♭)

E♭m

Minor

flametreemusic.com

Augmented

USEFUL

Chord Spelling

1st (E♭), 3rd (G), ♯5th (B)

E♭+

Augmented

flametreemusic.com

E♭°

Diminished

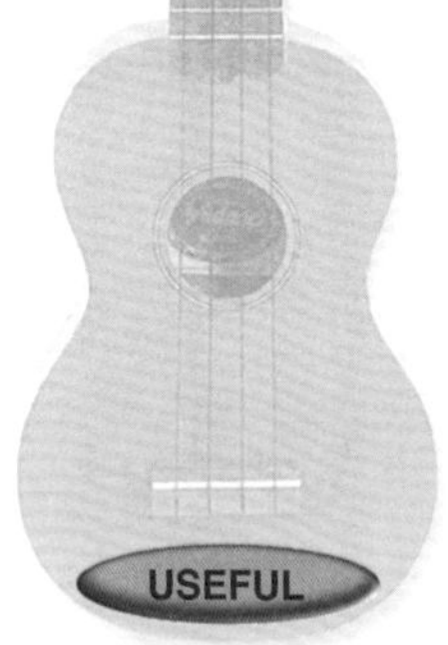

Chord Spelling

1st (E♭), ♭3rd (G♭), ♭5th (B♭♭)

E♭°

Diminished

B♭♭ E♭ G♭ B♭♭

flametreemusic.com

Start Here
A
B♭/A♯
B
C
C♯/D♭
D
E♭/D♯
E
F
F♯/G♭
G
A♭/G♯

E♭sus2

Suspended 2nd

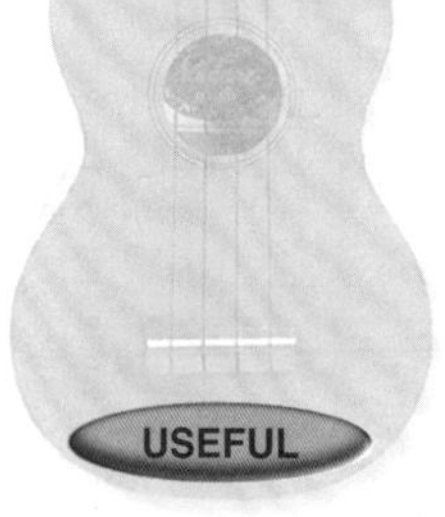

Chord Spelling

1st (E♭), 2nd (F), 5th (B♭)

E♭sus2

Suspended 2nd

A♭/G♯

Start Here
A
B♭/A#
B
C
C#/D♭
D
E♭/D#
E
F
F#/G♭
G
A♭/G#

E♭sus4

Suspended 4th

Chord Spelling

1st (E♭), 4th (A♭), 5th (B♭)

E♭sus4

Suspended 4th

B♭ E♭ A♭ B♭

Start Here
A
B♭/A♯
B
C
C♯/D♭
D
E♭/D♯
E
F
F♯/G♭
G
A♭/G♯

E♭6

Major 6th

Chord Spelling

1st (E♭), 3rd (G), 5th (B♭), 6th (C)

E♭6

Major 6th

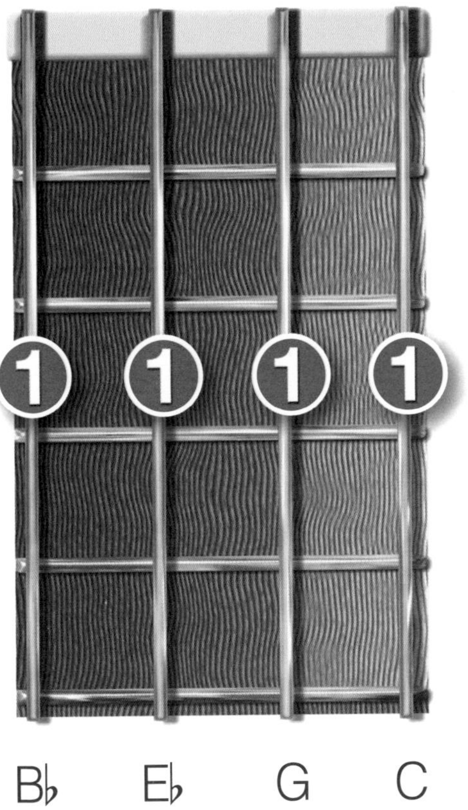

B♭ E♭ G C

Start Here
A
B♭/A♯
B
C

C♯/D♭
D

E♭/D♯

E
F

F♯/G♭
G

A♭/G♯

Start Here
A
B♭/A♯
B
C
C♯/D♭
D
E♭/D♯
E
F
F♯/G♭
G
A♭/G♯

E♭m6

Minor 6th

Chord Spelling

1st (E♭), ♭3rd (G♭), 5th (B♭), 6th (C

E♭m6

Minor 6th

flametreemusic.com

E♭6sus4

6th Suspended 4th

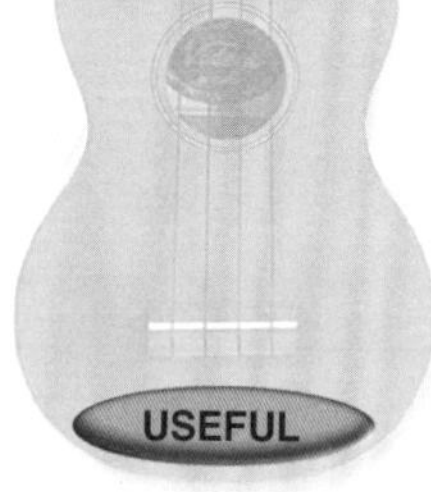

Chord Spelling

1st (E♭), 4th (A♭), 5th (B♭), 6th (C)

E♭6sus4

6th Suspended 4th

E♭maj7

Major 7th

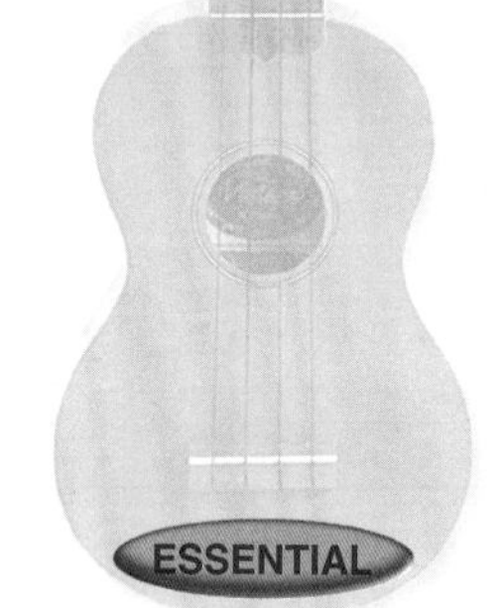

Chord Spelling

1st (E♭), 3rd (G), 5th (B♭), 7th (D)

E♭maj7

Major 7th

B♭ E♭ G D

Start Here
A
B♭/A♯
B
C
C♯/D♭
D
E♭/D♯
E
F
F♯/G♭
G
A♭/G♯

E♭m7

Minor 7th

Chord Spelling

1st (E♭), ♭3rd (G♭), 5th (B♭), ♭7th (D♭

E♭m7

Minor 7th

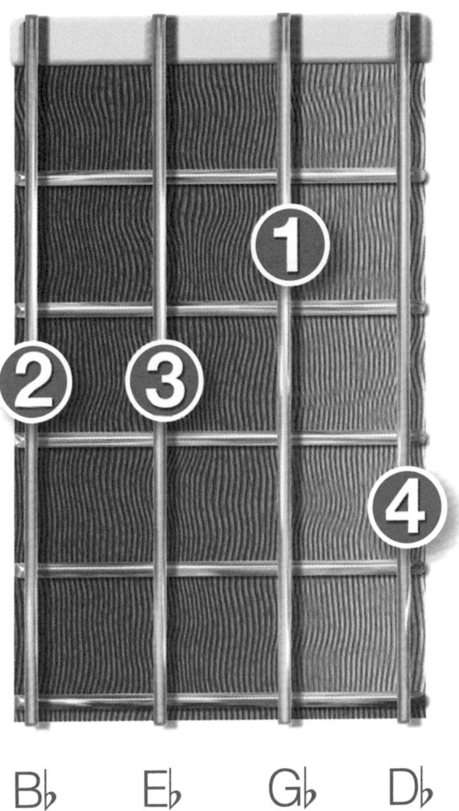

Start Here

A

B♭/A♯

B

C

C♯/D♭

D

E♭/D♯

E

F

F♯/G♭

G

A♭/G♯

E♭7

Dominant 7th

USEFUL

Chord Spelling

1st (E♭), 3rd (G), 5th (B♭), ♭7th (D♭)

E♭7

Dominant 7th

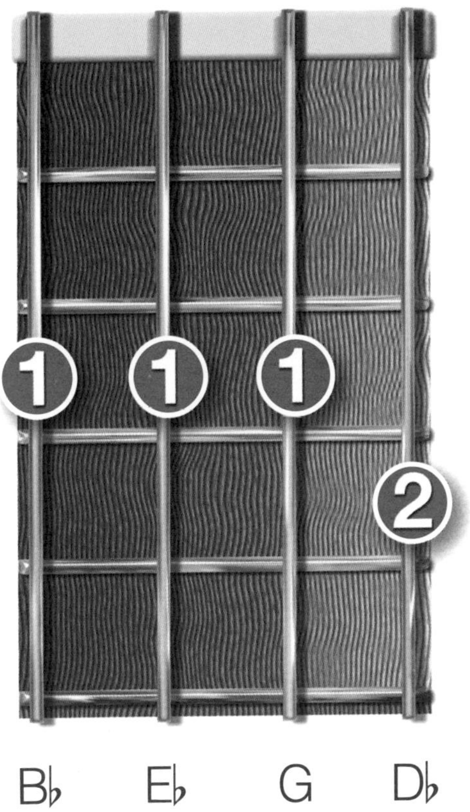

B♭ E♭ G D♭

E♭°7

Diminished 7th

OCCASIONAL

Chord Spelling

1st (E♭), ♭3rd (G♭), ♭5th (B𝄫), 𝄫7th (D𝄫

E♭°7

Diminished 7th

E♭7sus4

Dominant 7th Suspended 4th

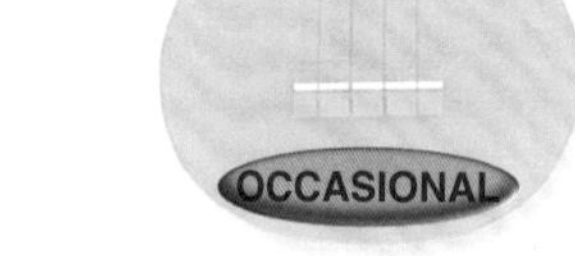

Chord Spelling

1st (E♭), 4th (A♭), 5th (B♭), ♭7th (D♭

E♭7sus4

Dominant 7th Suspended 4th

flametreemusic.com

Start Here
A
B♭/A♯
B
C
C♯/D♭
D
E♭/D♯
E
F
F♯/G♭
G

E♭/9

Major add 9th

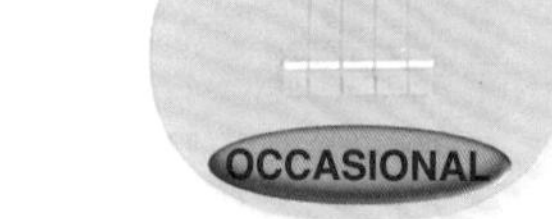

Chord Spelling

1st (E♭), 3rd (G), 5th (B♭), 9th (F)

E♭/9

Major add 9th

flametreemusic.com

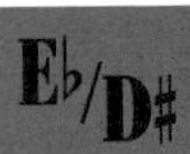

E

Major

Chord Spelling

1st (E), 3rd (G♯), 5th (B)

E

Major

Start Here
A
B♭/A♯
B
C
C♯/D♭
D
E♭/D♯
E
F
F♯/G♭
G
A♭/G♯

Em

Minor

Chord Spelling

1st (E), ♭3rd (G), 5th (B)

Em

Minor

flametreemusic.com

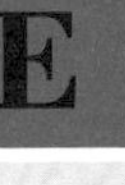

Start Here
A
B♭/A♯
B
C
C♯/D♭
D
E♭/D♯
E
F
F♯/G♭
G
A♭/G♯

E+
Augmented

Chord Spelling

1st (E), 3rd (G♯), ♯5th (B♯)

E+

Augmented

Start Here
A
B♭/A♯
B
C
C♯/D♭
D
E♭/D♯
E
F
F♯/G♭
G
A♭/G♯

E°

Diminished

Chord Spelling

1st (E), ♭3rd (G), ♭5th (B♭)

E°

Diminished

flametreemusic.com

Esus2

Suspended 2nd

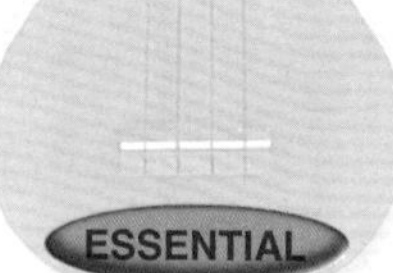

Chord Spelling

1st (E), 2nd (F♯), 5th (B)

Esus2

Suspended 2nd

flametreemusic.com

B♭/A♯
B
C
C♯/D♭
D
E♭/D♯
E
F
F♯/G♭
G
A♭/G♯

Start Here
A
B♭/A♯
B
C
C♯/D♭
D
E♭/D♯
E
F
F♯/G♭
G
A♭/G♯

Esus4

Suspended 4th

Chord Spelling

1st (E), 4th (A), 5th (B)

Esus4

Suspended 4th

flametreemusic.com

E6

Major 6th

Chord Spelling

1st (E), 3rd (G♯), 5th (B), 6th (C♯)

E6

Major 6th

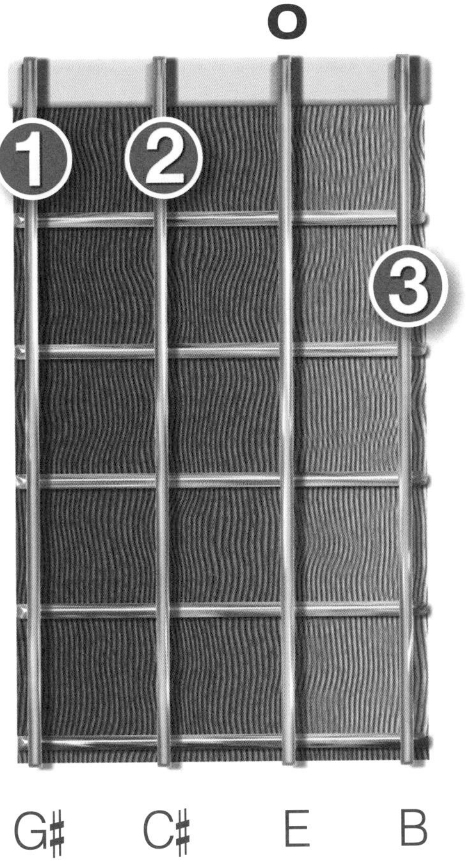
o
1
2
3
G♯ C♯ E B

Start Here
A
B♭/A♯
B

C
C♯/D♭
D

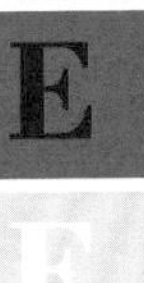
E♭/D♯
E

F
F♯/G♭
G
A♭/G♯

Em6

Minor 6th

Chord Spelling

1st (E), ♭3rd (G), 5th (B), 6th (C♯)

Em6

Minor 6th

flametreemusic.com

E6sus4

6th Suspended 4th

Chord Spelling

1st (E), 4th (A), 5th (B), 6th (C♯)

E6sus4

6th Suspended 4th

A C♯ E B

Start Here
A
B♭/A♯
B
C
C♯/D♭
D
E♭/D♯
E
F
F♯/G♭
G
A♭/G♯

Emaj7

Major 7th

Chord Spelling

1st (E), 3rd (G♯), 5th (B), 7th (D♯)

Emaj7

Major 7th

Start Here
A
B♭/A♯
B
C
C♯/D♭
D
E♭/D♯
E
F
F♯/G♭
G
A♭/G♯

Em7

Minor 7th

Chord Spelling

1st (E), ♭3rd (G), 5th (B), ♭7th (D)

Em7

Minor 7th

E7

Dominant 7th

USEFUL

Chord Spelling

1st (E), 3rd (G♯), 5th (B), ♭7th (D)

E7

Dominant 7th

Start Here
A
B♭/A♯
B
C
C♯/D♭
D
E♭/D♯
E
F
F♯/G♭
G
A♭/G♯

E°7 Diminished 7th

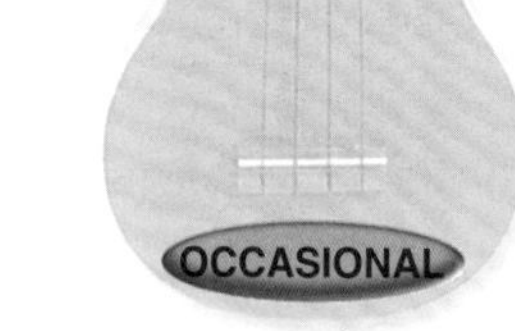

Chord Spelling

1st (E), ♭3rd (G), ♭5th (B♭), 𝄫7th (D♭)

E°7

Diminished 7th

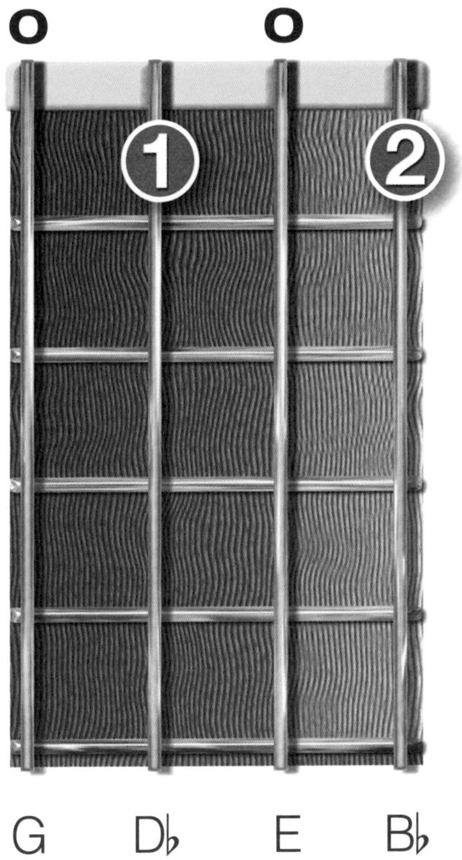

flametreemusic.com

Start Here

A

B♭/A♯

B

C

C♯/D♭

D

E♭/D♯

E

F

F♯/G♭

G

A♭/G♯

E7sus4

Dominant 7th Suspended 4th

Chord Spelling

1st (E), 4th (A), 5th (B), ♭7th (D)

E7sus4

Dominant 7th Suspended 4th

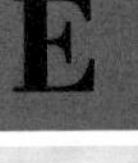

E/9

Major add 9th

Chord Spelling

1st (E), 3rd (G♯), 5th (B), 9th (F♯)

E/9

Major add 9th

G♯ E F♯ B

flametreemusic.com

Start Here
A
B♭/A♯
B
C
C♯/D♭
D
E♭/D♯
E
F
F♯/G♭
G
A♭/G♯

F Major

Chord Spelling

1st (F), 3rd (A), 5th (C)

F

Major

flametreemusic.com

Fm

Minor

ESSENTIAL

Chord Spelling

1st (F), ♭3rd (A♭), 5th (C)

Fm

Minor

flametreemusic.com

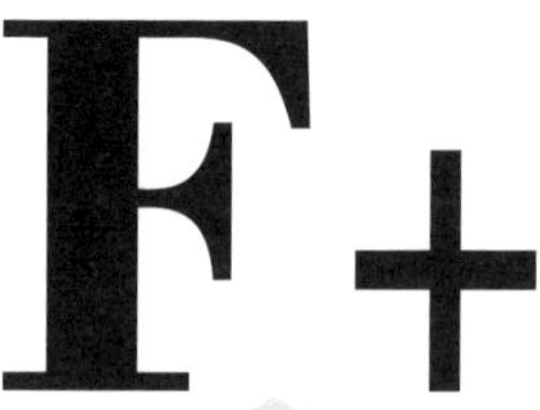

Augmented

Chord Spelling

1st (F), 3rd (A), ♯5th (C♯)

F+

Augmented

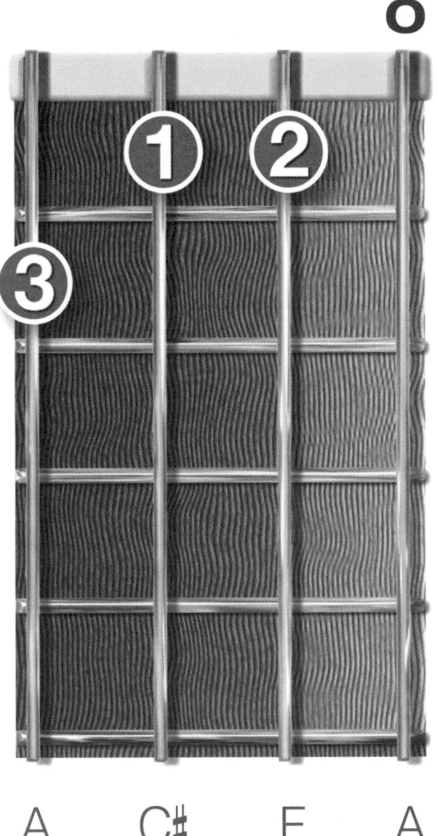

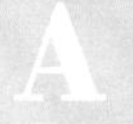
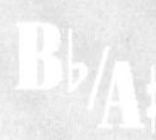
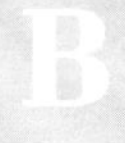

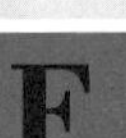
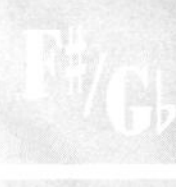
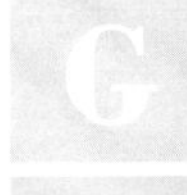
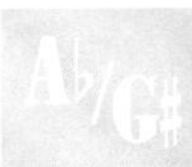

A C# F A

Start Here

A

B♭/A#

B

C

C#/D♭

D

E♭/D#

E

F#/G♭

G

A♭/G#

F°

Diminished

Chord Spelling

1st (F), ♭3rd (A♭), ♭5th (C♭)

F°

Diminished

Start Here
A
B♭/A♯
B
C
C♯/D♭
D
E♭/D♯
E
F
F♯/G♭
G
A♭/G♯

Fsus2

Suspended 2nd

Chord Spelling

1st (F), 2nd (G), 5th (C)

Fsus2

Suspended 2nd

flametreemusic.com

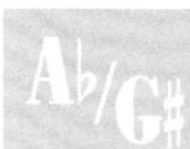

Fsus4

Suspended 4th

Chord Spelling

1st (F), 4th (B♭), 5th (C)

Fsus4

Suspended 4th

flametreemusic.com

F6

Major 6th

USEFUL

Chord Spelling

1st (F), 3rd (A), 5th (C), 6th (D)

F6

Major 6th

flametreemusic.com

Fm6

Minor 6th

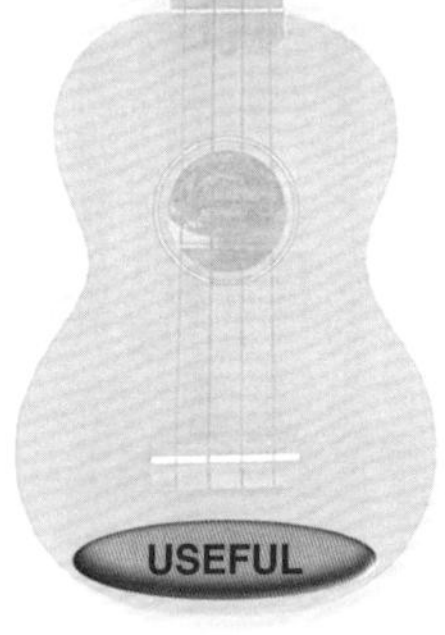

Chord Spelling

1st (F), ♭3rd (A♭), 5th (C), 6th (D)

Fm6

Minor 6th

A♭ D F C

flametreemusic.com

F6sus4

6th Suspended 4th

Chord Spelling

1st (F), 4th (B♭), 5th (C), 6th (D)

F6sus4

6th Suspended 4th

flametreemusic.com

Start Here
A
B♭/A♯
B
C
C♯/D♭
D
E♭/D♯
E
F

Fmaj7
Major 7th

Chord Spelling

1st (F), 3rd (A), 5th (C), 7th (E)

Fmaj7

Major 7th

Start Here
A
B♭/A♯
B
C
C♯/D♭
D
E♭/D♯
E
F
F♯/G♭
G
A♭/G♯

Fm7
Minor 7th

Chord Spelling

1st (F), ♭3rd (A♭), 5th (C), ♭7th (E♭)

Fm7

Minor 7th

Start Here

C

E

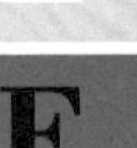

F7

Dominant 7th

OCCASIONAL

Chord Spelling

1st (F), 3rd (A), 5th (C), ♭7th (E♭)

F7

Dominant 7th

flametreemusic.com

Start Here
A
B♭/A♯
B
C
C♯/D♭
D
E♭/D♯
E
F
F♯/G♭
G
A♭/G♯

F°7

Diminished 7th

OCCASIONAL

Chord Spelling

1st (F), ♭3rd (A♭), ♭5th (C♭), ♭♭7th (E♭♭

F°7

Diminished 7th

flametreemusic.com

Start Here
A
B♭/A♯
B
C
C♯/D♭
D
E♭/D♯
E
F
F♯/G♭
G
A♭/G♯

F7sus4

Dominant 7th Suspended 4th

Chord Spelling

1st (F), 4th (B♭), 5th (C), ♭7th (E♭)

F7sus4

Dominated 7th Suspended 4th

B♭ E♭ F C

flametreemusic.com

F/9

Major add 9th

Chord Spelling

1st (F), 3rd (A), 5th (C), 9th (G)

F/9

Major add 9th

flametreemusic.com

Start Here
A
B♭/A♯
B
C
C♯/D♭
D
E♭/D♯
E
F
F♯/G♭
G
A♭/G♯

F♯ Major

Chord Spelling

1st (F♯), 3rd (A♯), 5th (C♯)

F♯

Major

A♯ C♯ F♯ A♯

Start Here
A
B♭/A♯
B
C
C♯/D♭
D
E♭/D♯
E
F
F♯/G♭
G

F♯m

Minor

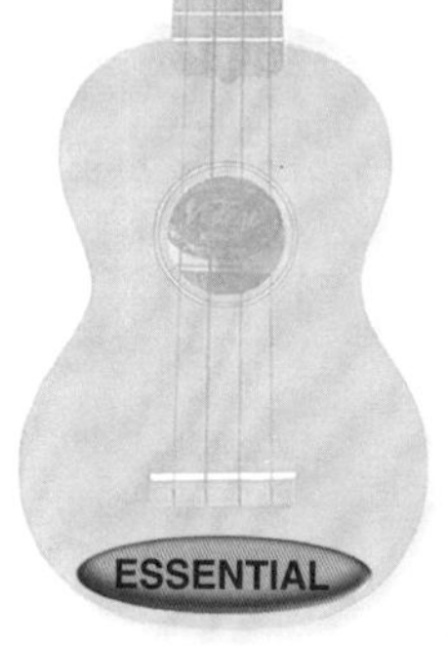

Chord Spelling

1st (F♯), ♭3rd (A), 5th (C♯)

F♯m

Minor

A C♯ F♯ A

flametreemusic.com

Augmented

USEFUL

Chord Spelling

1st (F♯), 3rd (A♯), ♯5th (Cx)

F♯+

Augmented

A♯ Cx F♯ A♯

flametreemusic.com

F♯°

Diminished

Chord Spelling

1st (F♯), ♭3rd (A), ♭5th (C)

F♯°

Diminished

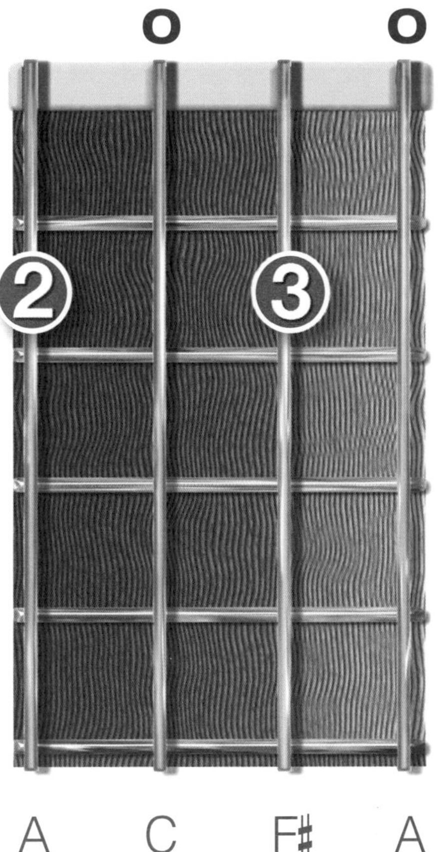

A C F♯ A

flametreemusic.com

Start Here
A
B♭/A♯
B
C
C♯/D♭
D
E♭/D♯
E
F
F♯/G♭
G
A♭/G♯

F♯sus2

Suspended 2nd

Chord Spelling

1st (F♯), 2nd (G♯), 5th (C♯)

F♯sus2

Suspended 2nd

G♯ C♯ F♯ C♯

flametreemusic.com

Start Here
A
B♭/A♯
B
C
C♯/D♭
D
E♭/D♯
E
F
F♯/G♭
G
A♭/G♯

F♯sus4

Suspended 4th

Chord Spelling

1st (F♯), 4th (B), 5th (C♯)

F♯sus4

Suspended 4th

B C♯ F♯ B

flametreemusic.com

F♯6

Major 6th

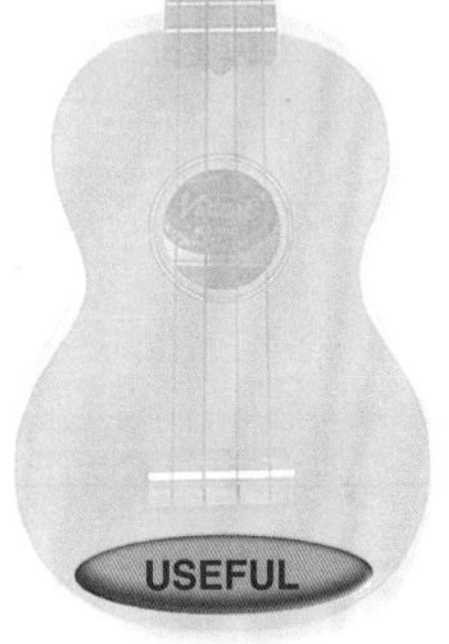

Chord Spelling

1st (F♯), 3rd (A♯), 5th (C♯), 6th (D♯

F♯6

Major 6th

A♯ D♯ F♯ C♯

flametreemusic.com

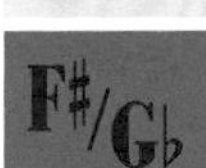

F♯m6

Minor 6th

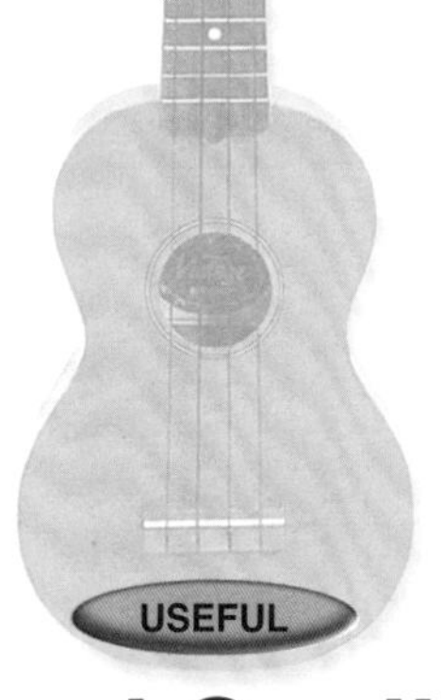

Chord Spelling

1st (F♯), ♭3rd (A), 5th (C♯), 6th (D♯

F♯m6

Minor 6th

A D♯ F♯ C♯

flametreemusic.com

Start Here
A
B♭/A♯
B
C
C♯/D♭
D
E♭/D♯
E
F
F♯/G♭
G
A♭/G♯

F♯6sus4

6th Suspended 4th

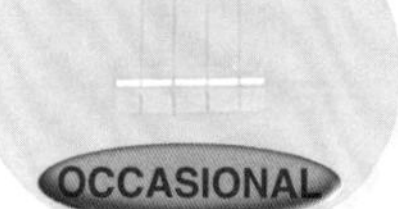

Chord Spelling

1st (F♯), 4th (B), 5th (C♯), 6th (D♯)

F♯6sus4

6th Suspended 4th

B D♯ F♯ C♯

flametreemusic.com

F♯maj7

Major 7th

Chord Spelling

1st (F♯), 3rd (A♯), 5th (C♯), 7th (E♯)

F♯maj7

Major 7th

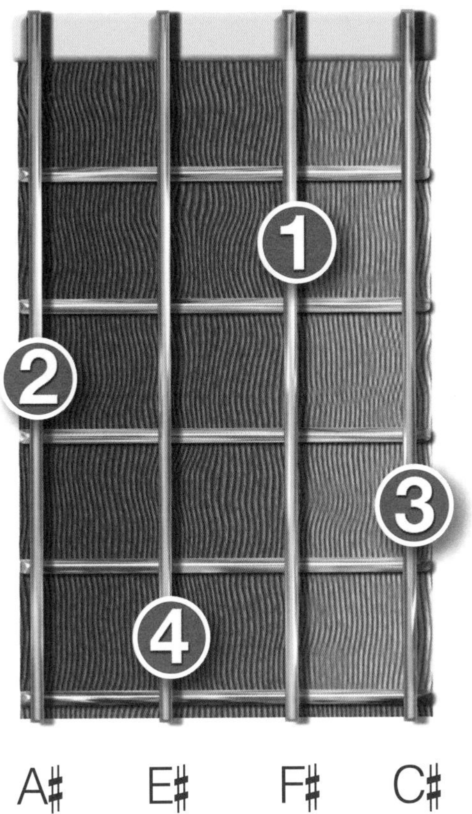

A♯ E♯ F♯ C♯

Start Here
A
B♭/A♯
B
C
C♯/D♭
D
E♭/D♯
E
F
F♯/G♭
G
A♭/G♯

F♯m7

Minor 7th

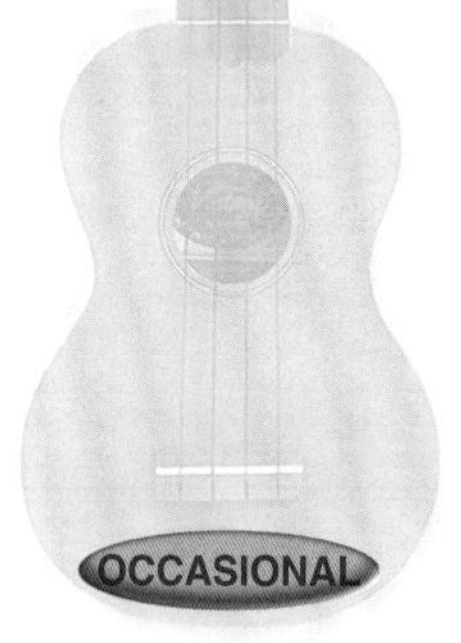

Chord Spelling

1st (F♯), ♭3rd (A), 5th (C♯), ♭7th (E)

F♯m7

Minor 7th

A E F♯ C♯

flametreemusic.com

F♯7

Dominant 7th

Chord Spelling

1st (F♯), 3rd (A♯), 5th (C♯), ♭7th (E)

F♯7

Dominant 7th

flametreemusic.com

Start Here
A
B♭/A♯
B
C
C♯/D♭
D
E♭/D♯
E
F

G
A♭/G♯

F♯°7

Diminished 7th

Chord Spelling

1st (F♯), ♭3rd (A), ♭5th (C), ♭♭7th (E♭

F♯°7

Diminished 7th

flametreemusic.com

Start Here
A
B♭/A♯
B
C
C♯/D♭
D
E♭/D♯
E
F
F♯/G♭
G
A♭/G♯

Start Here
A
B♭/A♯
B
C
C♯/D♭
D
E♭/D♯
E
F
F♯/G♭
G
A♭/G♯

F♯7sus4

Dominant 7th Suspended 4th

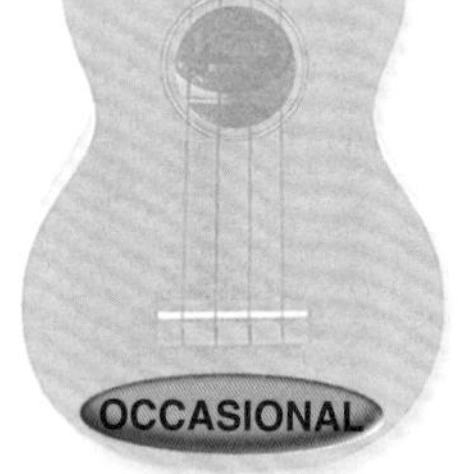

Chord Spelling

1st (F♯), 4th (B), 5th (C♯), ♭7th (E)

F♯7sus4

Dominant 7th Suspended 4th

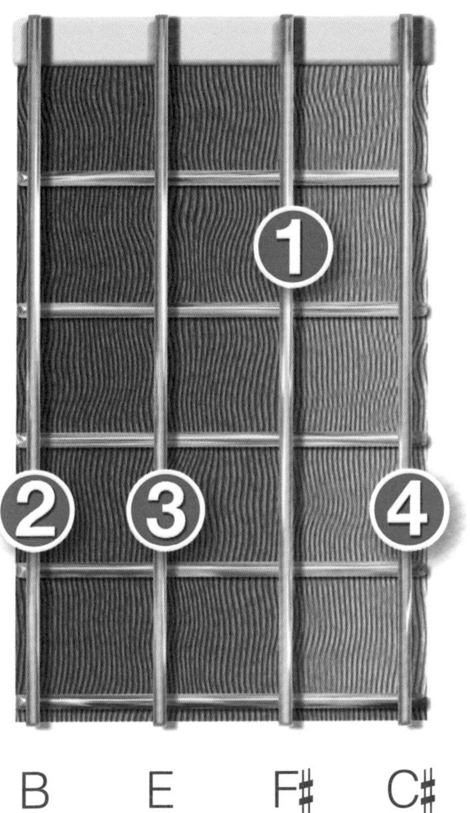

flametreemusic.com

Start Here
A
B♭/A♯
B
C
C♯/D♭
D
E♭/D♯
E
F
F♯/G♭
G
A♭/G♯

F♯/9

Major add 9th

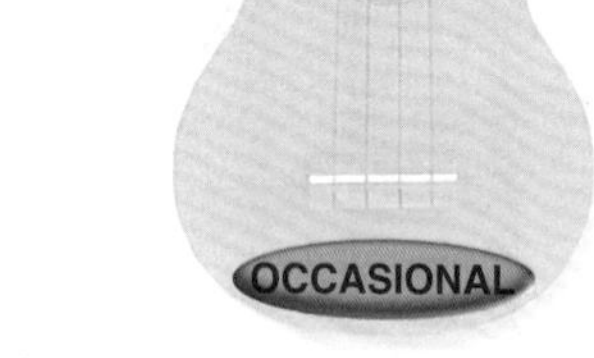

Chord Spelling

1st (F♯), 3rd (A♯), 5th (C♯), 9th (G♯

F♯/9

Major add 9th

G♯ C♯ F♯ A♯

flametreemusic.com

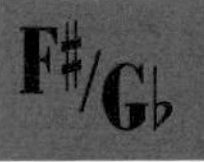

G Major

Chord Spelling

1st (G), 3rd (B), 5th (D)

G

Major

flametreemusic.com

Gm

Minor

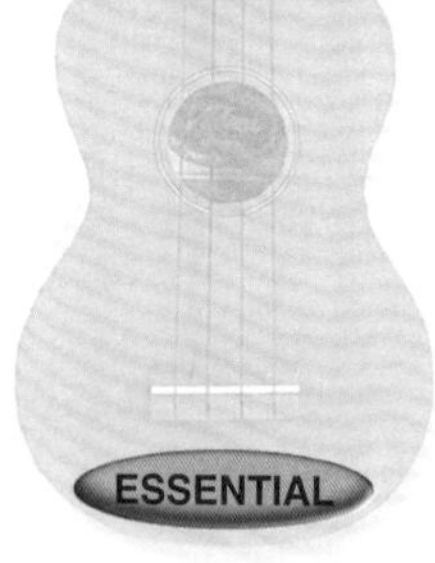

Chord Spelling

1st (G), ♭3rd (B♭), 5th (D)

Gm

Minor

G D G B♭

G+

Augmented

Chord Spelling

1st (G), 3rd (B), ♯5th (D♯)

G+

Augmented

Start Here
A
B♭/A♯
B
C
C♯/D♭
D
E♭/D♯
E
F
F♯/G♭
G
A♭/G♯

G°

Diminished

Chord Spelling

1st (G), ♭3rd (B♭), ♭5th (D♭)

G°

Diminished

Gsus2

Suspended 2nd

Chord Spelling

1st (G), 2nd (A), 5th (D)

Gsus2

Suspended 2nd

flametreemusic.com

C

E

Gsus4

Suspended 4th

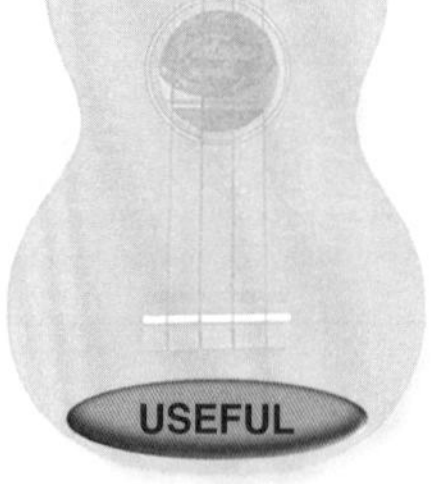

Chord Spelling

1st (G), 4th (C), 5th (D)

Gsus4

Suspended 4th

B♭/A♯
B
C
C♯/D♭
D
E♭/D♯
E
F
F♯/G♭
G
A♭/G♯

G6

Major 6th

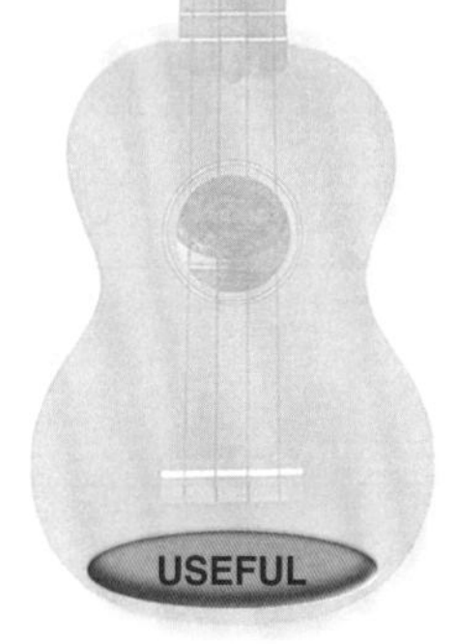

Chord Spelling

1st (G), 3rd (B), 5th (D), 6th (E)

G6

Major 6th

flametreemusic.com

Start Here
A
B♭/A♯
B
C
C♯/D♭
D
E♭/D♯
E
F
F♯/G♭
G
A♭/G♯

Gm6

Minor 6th

Chord Spelling

1st (G), ♭3rd (B♭), 5th (D), 6th (E

Gm6

Minor 6th

flametreemusic.com

Start Here
A
B♭/A♯
B
C
C♯/D♭
D
E♭/D♯
E
F
F♯/G♭
G

Start Here
A
B♭/A♯
B
C
C♯/D♭
D
E♭/D♯
E
F
F♯/G♭
G
A♭/G♯

G6sus4

6th Suspended 4th

Chord Spelling

1st (G), 4th (C), 5th (D), 6th (E)

G6sus4

6th Suspended 4th

Gmaj7

Major 7th

Chord Spelling

1st (G), 3rd (B), 5th (D), 7th (F♯)

Gmaj7

Major 7th

flametreemusic.com

Start Here

A

B♭/A♯

B

C

C♯/D♭

D

E♭/D♯

E

F

F♯/G♭

G

A♭/G♯

Gm7

Minor 7th

Chord Spelling

1st (G), ♭3rd (B♭), 5th (D), ♭7th (F)

Gm7

Minor 7th

Start Here

A

B♭/A♯

B

C

C♯/D♭

D

E♭/D♯

E

F

F♯/G♭

G

A♭/G♯

G7 Dominant 7th

Chord Spelling

1st (G), 3rd (B), 5th (D), ♭7th (F)

G7

Dominant 7th

G°7

Diminished 7th

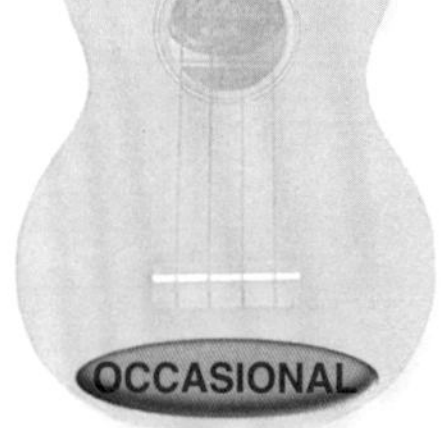

Chord Spelling

1st (G), ♭3rd (B♭), ♭5th (D♭), 𝄫7th (F♭)

G°7

Diminished 7th

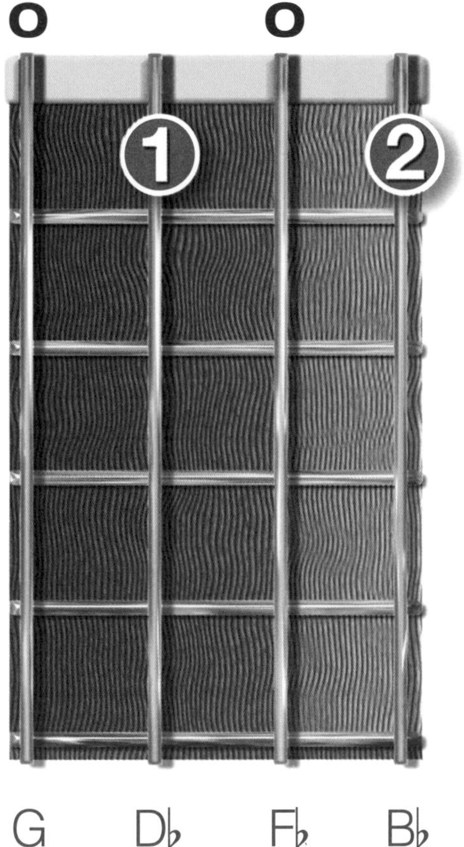

G D♭ F♭ B♭

flametreemusic.com

Start Here
A
B♭/A♯
B
C
C♯/D♭
D
E♭/D♯
E
F
F♯/G♭
G
A♭/G♯

G7sus4

Dominant 7th Suspended 4th

Chord Spelling

1st (G), 4th (C), 5th (D), ♭7th (F)

G7sus4

Dominant 7th Suspended 4th

G/9

Major add 9th

Chord Spelling

1st (G), 3rd (B), 5th (D), 9th (A)

G/9

Major add 9th

flametreemusic.com

Start Here
A
B♭/A#
B
C
C#/D♭
D
E♭/D#
E
F
F#/G♭
G
A♭/G#

A♭ Major

Chord Spelling

1st (A♭), 3rd (C), 5th (E♭)

A♭

Major

A♭ E♭ A♭ C

flametreemusic.com

A♭m Minor

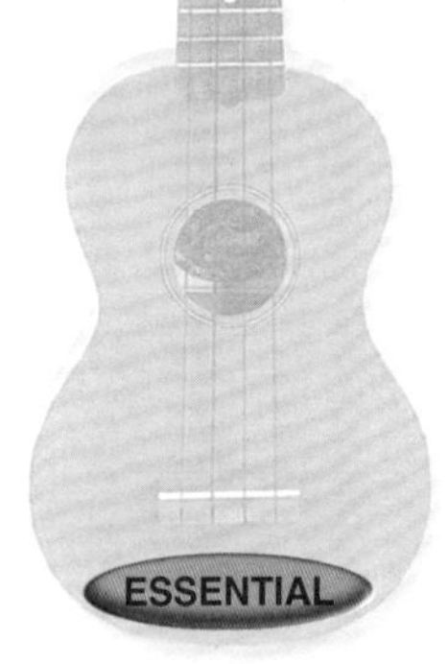

Chord Spelling

1st (A♭), ♭3rd (C♭), 5th (E♭)

A♭m

Minor

Start Here
A
B♭/A♯
B
C
C♯/D♭
D
E♭/D♯
E
F
F♯/G♭
G
A♭/G♯

Start Here
A
B♭/A#
B
C
C#/D♭
D
E♭/D#
E
F
F#/G♭
G
A♭/G#

A♭+

Augmented

USEFUL

Chord Spelling

1st (A♭), 3rd (C), ♯5th (E)

A♭+

Augmented

flametreemusic.com

Start Here
A
B♭/A#
B
C
C#/D♭
D
E♭/D#
E
F
F#/G♭
G
A♭/G#

Diminished

Chord Spelling

1st (A♭), ♭3rd (C♭), ♭5th (E♭♭)

A♭°

Diminished

A♭ E♭♭ A♭ C♭

flametreemusic.com

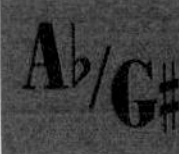

Start Here
A
B♭/A♯
B
C
C♯/D♭
D
E♭/D♯
E
F
F♯/G♭
G
A♭/G♯

A♭sus2

Suspended 2nd

Chord Spelling

1st (A♭), 2nd (B♭), 5th (E♭)

A♭sus2

Suspended 2nd

A♭ E♭ A♭ B♭

A♭sus4

Suspended 4th

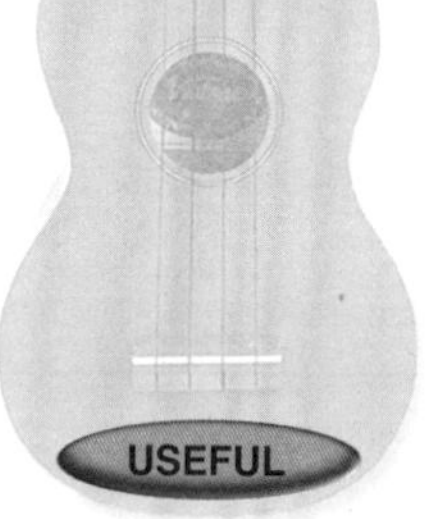

Chord Spelling

1st (A♭), 4th (D♭), 5th (E♭)

A♭sus4

Suspended 4th

A♭ E♭ A♭ D♭

flametreemusic.com

A♭6

Major 6th

Chord Spelling

1st (A♭), 3rd (C), 5th (E♭), 6th (F)

A♭6

Major 6th

Start Here
A
B♭/A#
B
C
C#/D♭
D
E♭/D#
E
F
F#/G♭
G
A♭/G#

A♭m6
Minor 6th

Chord Spelling

1st (A♭), ♭3rd (C♭), 5th (E♭), 6th (F

A♭m6

Minor 6th

A♭6sus4

6th Suspended 4th

Chord Spelling

1st (A♭), 4th (D♭), 5th (E♭), 6th (F)

A♭6sus4

6th Suspended 4th

A♭ E♭ F D♭

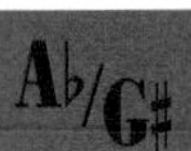

Start Here
A
B♭/A♯
B
C
C♯/D♭
D
E♭/D♯
E
F
F♯/G♭
G
A♭/G♯

Chord Spelling

1st (A♭), 3rd (C), 5th (E♭), 7th (G

A♭maj7

Major 7th

flametreemusic.com

Start Here
A
B♭/A♯
B
C
C♯/D♭
D
E♭/D♯
E
F
F♯/G♭
G
A♭/G♯

A♭m7
Minor 7th

Chord Spelling

1st (A♭), ♭3rd (C♭), 5th (E♭), ♭7th (G♭

A♭m7

Minor 7th

A♭7 Dominant 7th

Chord Spelling

1st (A♭), 3rd (C), 5th (E♭), ♭7th (G♭)

A♭7

Dominant 7th

flametreemusic.com

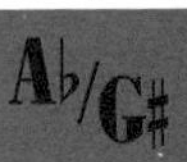

Start Here
A
B♭/A#
B
C
C#/D♭
D
E♭/D#
E
F
F#/G♭
G
A♭/G#

A♭°7 Diminished 7th

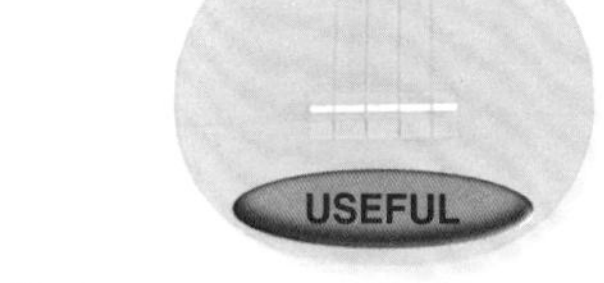

Chord Spelling

1st (A♭), ♭3rd (C♭), ♭5th (E♭♭), ♭♭7th (G♭♭

A♭°7

Diminished 7th

A♭ E♭♭ G♭♭ C♭

flametreemusic.com

A♭7sus4

Dominant 7th Suspended 4th

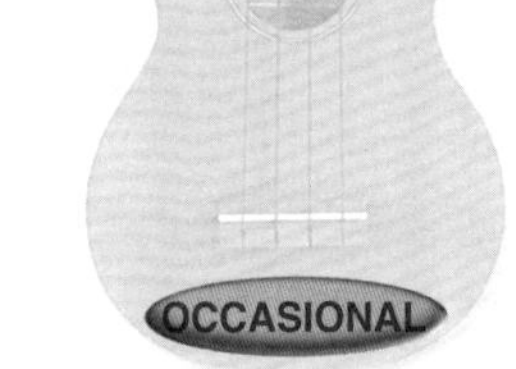

Chord Spelling

1st (A♭), 4th (D♭), 5th (E♭), 7th (G♭)

A♭7sus4

Dominant 7th Suspended 4th

Start Here
A
B♭/A♯
B
C
C♯/D♭
D
E♭/D♯
E
F
F♯/G♭
G
A♭/G♯

A♭/9

Major add 9th

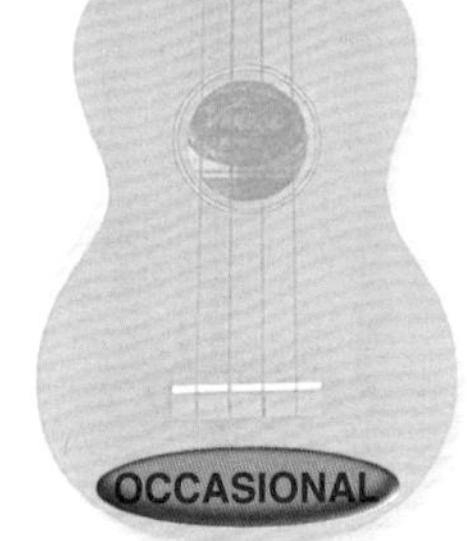

Chord Spelling

1st (A♭), 3rd (C), 5th (E♭), 9th (B♭)

A♭/9

Major add 9th

B♭ E♭ A♭ C

flametreemusic.com

Further Reading and other useful internet resources for this book are available on **www.flametreemusic.com**

Simple Ukulele Chords is another in our best-selling series of easy-to-use music books designed for players of all abilities and ages. Created for musicians by musicians, these books offer a quick and practical resource for those playing on their own or with a band. They work equally well for the rock and indie musician as they do for the jazz, folk, country, blues or classical enthusiast.

FlameTreeMusic.com

Practical information on chords, scales, riffs, rhymes and instruments through a growing combination of traditional print books and ebooks. Features over **1800** chords, 240 scales, with **piano** and **guitar sounds** for every chord.

Books in the series:

Advanced Guitar Chords; Beginner's Guide to Reading Music; Piano & Keyboard Chords; Chords for Kids; Play Flamenco; How to Play Guitar; How to Play Bass Guitar; How to Play Piano; How to Play Classic Riffs; Songwriter's Rhyming Dictionary; How to Become a Star; How to Read Music; How to Write Great Songs; How to Play Rock Rhythm, Riffs & Lead; How to Play Hard, Metal & Nu Rock; How to Make Music on the Web; My First Recorder Music; Piano Sheet Music; Brass & Wind Sheet Music; Scales & Modes.

For further information on these titles please visit our trading website: www.flametreepublishing.com